I0756847

NEEDLESS SUFFERING
But why?

LUIS MASHAPURE

authorHOUSE®

AuthorHouse™ UK
1663 Liberty Drive
Bloomington, IN 47403 USA
www.authorhouse.co.uk
Phone: 0800 047 8203 (Domestic TFN)
        +44 1908 723714 (International)

Published by AuthorHouse 08/30/2019

ISBN: 978-1-7283-8639-3 (sc)
ISBN: 978-1-7283-8640-9 (e)

THE AUTHOR

In writing this book, the author - Luis Mashapure - was driven by passion in helping communities transform themselves from dependency to self-sufficiency through collective effort by setting up Community Commonwealth Projects. Luis, in this first of a two-part series, investigates the nature and circumstances of the poor majority in society.

Luis did his primary education at Maqkwau and Chikangwe Primary Schools of Hurungwe district of Zimbabwe in the late seventies. He enrolled for secondary education at the sole privately-run Catholic School - St Paul's - in Karoi, Zim. Luis went on to teach at Hesketh Park School (1983-84) and Pote Primary School (1985) in the rank of 'teacher awaiting training'. However, instead of moving into the teaching field, Luis - by Sept 1985 - went for Agriculture Training at Essexvale Institute of Agriculture (Esigodini) in Bulawayo, Zimbabwe. Thereafter Luis joined the Department of Agriculture, Research and Extension Services [AGRITEX] by Aug 1987, as an Agricultural Technician in Makoni District of Zimbabwe.

By 1990 Luis enrolled at the coveted Gwebi College of Agriculture for a Higher National Diploma in Agriculture after which he rejoined AGRITEX as an Agricultural Extension Officer (AEO) in Mash Central Province. 1994 saw Luis take a bold move into the private sector and joined a blue-chip corporate organisation - Windmill Pvt Ltd – as Regional Sales Agronomist. From 1998 until 2001, Luis successfully studied for a BSc in Agriculture [Management] (BSCAM) at the University of Zimbabwe. Still anchored in Windmill Pvt Ltd, Luis cracked on until 2004 when he resigned to set up his own agribusiness – Turbonet Pvt Ltd.

In 2005 Luis immigrated to the United Kingdom together with his family. In UK he earned an MBA at The University of Huddersfield and worked under various organisations – in Private Sector, Local Government and also in the Public Service in various role capacities. Luis is married to Sarudzai – a Nursing Practitioner (NHS) and has two daughters, Thelma and Tiana.

DEDICATION

This book is dedicated to contemporary thinkers of our time – candid, brave and selfless people whose critical voices are helping reshape our world for the better.

These are man, women and our youths of all colours and creed, who are taking painstaking effort to find answers to the scourge of poverty and needless suffering of billions of innocent people.

For the Sake of Posterity

Acknowledgement

Matthew Mtungambera, a dear friend and cousin of mine encouraged me to share my ideas and vision on eradication of hunger and poverty on the face of the planet.

I grew up with this guy up-to our mid-teens in the rural area of Chundu, in Hurungwe District of Zimbabwe. We both relocated to Harare, the sunshine capital city of Zimbabwe and other places, in pursuit of higher education and professional training.

We both struggled to make breakthroughs in education because of the skewed nature of resource distribution in Africa. 'Miraculously', Matthew went on to be a high-flyer, highly qualified Health Delivery Service practitioner in Indianapolis, USA, while I settled for an Executive Role in the multidisciplinary Operational Delivery Profession (ODP) in the UK's Public Service.

Matthew, thanks for the support and encouragement. It's all done! God Bless!

CONTENTS

Preface

The common characterisation of many countries of the world, especially those of Africa, is in terms of corruption, poor governance and misplaced priorities. Invariably, the obscene levels of poverty in society remain glaringly unpleasant to all. Despite all the efforts, the scourge of poverty continues to rise unabated. In a perfect world mankind should be telling stories of how successive and continuous generations benefit from sustainable exploitation of material resources, the capital fund and the productive forces that is handed down to all people by previous generations. Disturbingly, however, this is far from the case as resource distribution is sharply skewed in favour of the rich, oligarchs, and the politically connected.

Disruptive innovations appear to be the best approach to confront and conquer poverty. The writer blends his ideas and reflections on the scourge of poverty with contributions from a wide range of people that include workers, professionals, scholars and global commentators on development. The final view point turns out to be a 'black-hole' in which whoever gets into it, will never come out. It's because when sound minds understand perils of poverty, there is no rest till the elusive solution is found.

The prevalence of elitism in the global political sphere and emergence of predatory capitalist systems in the west and Marxist dictatorships in Africa, Asia, Latin America and elsewhere, has become a cause of concern as this phenomenon is responsible for dragging the global community into a vicious cycle of relentless poverty and needless suffering.

CHAPTER ONE

COLOUR OF THE HUMAN MIND

Introduction

One may ask, 'Is it possible to end hunger and suffering on earth?' If history be our judge, it would be correct to say that there is no precise answer – both 'yes' and 'no' are possible answers. But the truth of the matter is that suffering is needless in a world of plenty with abundant fresh air, water, fish, vegetation, minerals - you name it; we have it all.

We simply need to manage these God given resources equitably and sustainably.

Despite unprecedented advances in science and technology which should otherwise be enabling highest levels of food production, creation of jobs etc., and inspite of medical advances that should be guaranteeing longevity and decent standards of living, mankind's wickedness always raises the spectra of hunger and needless suffering. For *example, nations continue to vilify, hating and pouring scorn upon one another. Meanwhile, super-powers stick to their nuclear arsenals and deadly missile systems which can accidentally break loose, thus causing a biblical Herculean Armageddon.*

Some blame failed communist policies while others castigate the predatory nature of capitalism as the precursor of our problems. Those standing in between think the real cause is greed which nourishes and sustains oligarchs and dictatorships. Capitalist barons bribe governments and go on to spark senseless wars between nations. Innocent citizens are forced to pay for these wars, while behind the scenes, they rake billions from their investments in the military hardware industry. This is the shameless Colour of the human mind.

The relentless suffering of the peoples of the world has left philosophers and philanthropists dumbfounded. A few have turned to the bible for answers leaving majority clueless. Perplexing in deed and akin to the story of the Israelites getting stranded in the wilderness for 40 years - enduring hunger, disillusionment and disorientation but finally making it into the promised land – a land of milk and honey. Humanity needs a leap of faith to believe poverty can be eliminated.

We shouldn't lose hope. "For I know the plans I have for you" – so declares the Lord. "Plans to prosper you and not to harm you. Plans to give you hope and a future" - Jeremiah 29:11. The awesome power of the Lord is revealed in the second part in this series when we look at how hopelessness can be traded for true emancipation.

Candid Facts

The New Internationalist Independent Media organisation published an article (Poor and Rich, the facts [March 1999]) in which it observed that :–

'The world's 225 richest people have a combined wealth of over $1million million ($1trillion). Only four per cent of this wealth – $40 billion – would be enough for basic education and healthcare, adequate food and safe water and sanitation for the entire global population (https://newint.org/features/1999/03/01/poor-rich-the-facts/)'

Historical perspectives

Gubhuuu-uuh! Gubhuu-u-uu! Tsvoo-oh! Twaa-aa-twaa-oh! Such was the sound of heavy artillery fire which marked the start of World War Two (WW2). History tells us that the first victim was Poland while the rest followed. Lethal bombs and multiple rocket launchers were used to subdue opponents.

Historians will further tell us that the Blitzkrieg strategy by the NAZI, characterized by relentless bombings to destroy the enemy's air capacity, railroads, communications lines etc., had an enduring global impact on the lives of the people. The post WW2 settlement (by the League of Nations) created the new world order which has largely stood to this day. However, the barbaric war altered all norms of civilised cooperation between countries.

Oblivious to the writing on the wall, Hitler envisioned great victory in WW2.

We now all know that Hitler's carnage precursed the creation of an opposing force – the 'Allied Nations' which comprised of more than fifty countries including USA, USSR, France, Great Brittan and many of the latter's former colonies - the likes of Australia, Canada, New Zealand, South Africa, Kenya etc. Hitler forged alliances with forces of evil, the so-called Axis Powers comprising of Italy, Japan and others. A handful remained neutral.

Ironically and despite the devasting effects of the WW2, some scholars have come up with a critique revealing some positive aspects of the war. The debate lives on.

By far, this was the greatest of all wars ever fought on the face of the planet. It drew into its vortex more than sixty countries. The total death toll was a staggering 60 million people of which

 Needless Suffering

40ml were civilians. It was a war of attrition in which man and women fought against evil for the sake of their children's future. The Hitlerites sought to defeat the world and create a world dominated by what they called 'pure and superior race', following the ill-conceived, poorly understood flawed theory of Eugenics. On the other hand, the Allies fought against what they saw as pure evil and as such a war of survival of mankind. By shear Grace, after six years of brutal warfare (1939-1945), the Allied forces emerged victorious.

The Scourge of Our Time

In parallel dimensions lie the battle of our time – fighting poverty. We can safely describe it as a war between the poor and the rich because, generally speaking, the wealthy do not want to share their wealth with the poor. But why?

Most developing countries, especially former colonies, are generally poor and cannot provide enough for their citizens' basic needs (food, health and education services). Rich countries e.g. UK or France suffer yawning inequality gaps between their peoples. However, these countries cushion their less privileged citizens by availing such schemes as Income Support, Housing Benefits, Food Stamps etc. Such schemes, however, are either inadequate or non-existent in poor countries.

CHAPTER TWO

CONTEMPORARY PERSPECTIVES

Hard facts from contemporary perspectives suggest that mankind ought to wage a global war on poverty, hunger and social insecurity, the same way allied forces fought the axis forces of evil.

According to Oxfam pre-Devon 2018 Report (https://oxfamapps.org/media/press_release/2017-01-eight-people-own-same-wealth-as-half-the-world/), the gap between the richest and the poor people is greater than feared. Eight billionaires own the same wealth as 3.6 billion people who form the poorest half of the world's population.

Oxfam's report revealed that in 2015 the world's richest one percent retained their share of global wealth and still owned more than the other 99 percent combined. This concentration of wealth at the top held back the fight to end global poverty.

The report describes how the inequality crisis is being fueled by companies whose business models favour shareholders and top executives while paying little or no regard to workers or society in general. Companies increasingly focus on delivering ever higher returns to wealthy owners. Their businesses are structured to dodge taxes while driving down workers' wages. Even producers are not paid fair prices for their produce.

Against the backdrop of this report, the quest for 'Responsible leadership' has become ever more imperative. It's becoming increasingly necessary that economic management fundamentals are changed to benefit everyone, not just a privileged few.

Mark Goldring, Oxfam GB Chief Executive, once lamented: 'It is beyond grotesque that a group of men who could easily fit in a single golf buggy own more wealth than the poorest half of humanity, while one in nine people on the planet will go to bed hungry, every day'.

The fact that a super-rich elite class can prosper at the expense of the rest of us at home and overseas shows how warped our socio-economic principles have become. Inequality is keeping millions of people trapped in poverty while at the same time fracturing societies and poisoning our politics. Mark quipped, 'Sadly, top executives take home massive bonuses while workers' wages stagnate. Millionaires dodge taxes when public services are being cut'.

Of course, yes. For example, we see this in bloated government officials and local authorities' executives' pecks which are unjustifiably huge at the expense of service delivery to the people. No wonder why they serve as gatekeepers of the bad system.

The report, however, acknowledges that, while the number of people living in extreme poverty has decreased in recent decades, 700ml more could have escaped poverty if action had been taken to reduce the gap between the rich and poor.

Experts, including the World Bank and the International Monetary Fund, warn that further progress is under threat because of inequality.

Clearly, we see need for more human economy where markets - a vital engine for prosperity - are better managed to ensure no one is left out or denied basic rights such as decent work, healthcare and education.

Critical action steps, as reported, would include the following: -

- Improved cooperation between governments to prevent tax dodging that

     Needless Suffering

costs poor countries at least $100 billion every year;

- *Government action to encourage companies to act more for the benefit of their workforces and wider society;*
- *Taxes on wealth to generate funds for healthcare, education and job creation;*
- *Tackling the barriers that hold back women including lack of education opportunities and the burden of unpaid care work.*

The global poverty phenomenon has given rise to the mushrooming of donors, NGOs, Philanthropists etc., all purporting to be driven by need to help the poor. Some propagate sustainable programmes while others' services are a scratch on the surface of poverty. Perhaps it serves to show the scale of challenge we face in fighting poverty.

It goes without saying that this is the reason why Dambisa Moyo of Zambia claims that some of the so-called AID, is in effect the greatest cause of poverty. Much of the AID is largely tied to the goals of the AID organisations, some of whom are bent on promoting their sponsors' agendas as opposed to working whole-heartedly to eradicate poverty.

Progressive people can now see that poverty should be fought at all levels. The desire by the rich to keep on amassing wealth, albeit at the expense of the poor majority, is mind- boggling.

Just as spirited as the warlords of WW2 were in their assault of the free world, so are the rich and supper rich of our globalized world against the helpless poor. They bribe governments to win their way into fatty contracts whose eventual services do not match the sums they are paid.

In Africa and the other regions of developing countries, corporates and their western governments have used donors as agents to help them penetrate and exploit resources of poor countries. This has been vividly shown in a TEDx talk in Berlin by Mallence Bart-Williams (https://www.youtube.com/watch?v=AfnruW7yERA). The highly gifted speaker emphatically tells of how some donors give so little to the poor while behind the scenes they facilitate the syphoning of huge amounts of wealth from these unsuspecting countries.

Today, it is believed that hegemonic practices by the early western settlers in the Americas influenced many dictators around the world to run their countries with an iron fist. Unfortunately, our children aren't getting adequate enlightenment on this evil so that they can learn from mankind's past mistakes to shape the future for the better.

CHAPTER THREE

ROOT CAUSES OF POVERTY

Background

Over centuries, perhaps from start of African slavery, more than 350 years ago to this day, problems stem from the fact that our leaders are greedy, selfish and inept. In their true form they would rather be dictatorial than democratic. Instead of allowing people to use their talents and invest in socio-economic projects, they create conditions of impossibilities and would rather give away large swathes of land and other resources to foreigners (who give kick-backs) at the expense of their people.

Modern day philanthropy focuses not only on staving off hunger and poverty among the poor, but also helping them stand on their own feet by pursuing Social Enterprises.

Various reasons are cited as causes of poverty in different regions of the world. Good examples in

African countries is that of slavery and colonialism which have been responsible for poverty and disempowerment. Misgovernance and greed of leaders have been cited as other causes of poor government performance.

Various commentators have reported evidence of colonialists devising ways of reversing African civilization and subduing them, in order to steal their wealth.

Pioneer colonialists found the people of Africa well organised and culturally intertwined and focused on their march towards civilization. Imagine for hundreds of years (since around C250BC) they had mastered the technology to smelt iron. This was disrupted by both slavery and colonialism. Colonialists' insatiable appetite for resources became the precursor for the partition of Africa following the Berlin Conference of 1884-85.

The irony of the whole matter is that, if the enslavers and colonialists had the wisdom to join hands with natives, to jointly exploit resources for the good of mankind, a lot of positive things could have been achieved and abundance peace and tranquility could have prevailed. This could have been a precursor for great achievements. But, alas! The devil wouldn't allow that. On the contrary, people from former colonies of Africa, Asia and Latin America were viewed as inferior and in some instances, sub-human. Against this

		Needless Suffering

backdrop emerged the dark spirit of Eugenics in western countries. This spirit was so ugly and yet powerful - so much so that - it blind-folded every explorer, slave dealer or colonialist alike. They ended up committing all the associated crimes against humanity as we know them today.

The colonialists killed innocent people and more so the native leaders in order to exploit resources without interruption. This is how 'predatory capitalism' was founded. Even when a semblance of normalcy returned by the end of the 20th century, no moral commitment has been demonstrated to pay reparations for these crimes. Ironically, Hitlerites were made to pay for their WW2 sins; that money of course changing hands in Europe. Those slave masters who lost businesses in slave trading were compensated handsomely in America and Europe. In the US, the proposed pittance assistance of 40 acres and a donkey or mule to each freed slave was harshly reversed, leaving those freed from the yoke of slavery, vulnerable and at the mercy of poverty claws.

Imagine eating an apple-pie with sand mixture? Would you enjoy it? Difficult! This is what we see today in the western world. They have their pie which looks very delicious, but they can't eat it. In other words, Europe and the western capitalists cannot enjoy what they have as much as they should. They need to redeem themselves by paying reparations for their indulgence in the slave trade.

It would be profound and remarkable to see America and former European champions of the Trans-Atlantic slave trade settle their moral obligation debt to Africans who are answering the call to return home to Africa and those remaining. The same would apply to the Caribbean, Latin America and mainland Africa, who suffered the brunt of slavery and colonialism – and are still licking the wounds to this day. Ideally, no push would be necessary; perpetrators simply need to own-up to their obligations - as a generational responsibility - while realizing that redemptive reparations are a spiritual, social and legal imperative. Perhaps, like all other setbacks endured by people the world-over, the Mediterranean disasters of innocent Africans trying to escape poverty, tyranny and sponsored dictatorships, may cease and Africa will, in earnest, open its bowl of resources to the world for equitably shared prosperity.

Much of Africa, India, Chile, Peru, Brazil and many other regions or countries that once experienced slavery or colonialism or both are ready to forgive those who accept wrong doing and apologize. Accepting responsibility frees the mind from guilt of wrong-doing. In the absence of moral acts, only a false sense of happiness prevails.

    Needless Suffering

Historical tradition talks of the sobering words of former Emperor Haile Selassie of Ethiopia following the 1923 failed attempt by the League of Nations, which Ethiopia had joined, to stop Italy from invading Ethiopia.

As Italy bulldozed its way upon Ethiopia, the emperor appealed for help from western countries. The answer was, 'defend yourself'. This was obviously unthinkable given Italy outsmarted Ethiopia vastly in every respect including militarily and economically. Simply put, the western world did not have the moral drive to help. Then, in what became prophetic words, the Emperor told the west that one day it would be themselves facing military adventurism from powerful rogue states. True to his words, it took just a few years for the devastating barbaric WW2 to break out in Europe, in 1939. The consequences were herculean, to say the least.

History has the notoriety of repeating itself. Today, African citizens are crying out to the west to help in ending dictatorships in Africa by using its civilized influence through AU or UN. The west has enough experience and resources to do this. But what do we see? No action but leap service only. It demonstrates how immoral people are. No one knows why for sure.

All the while, thousands continue to die in the Mediterranean Sea as they try to escape horrendous dictatorships of Africa. Rigged elections across Africa - in Kenya, DRC, Congo, Eq. Guinea etc., have caused untold suffering and economic regression. Ironically, we continue to witness multinational corporations enjoying super wealth under these circumstances.

In the 'Biblical Perspectives' by Ted Hayes [Sept 2004], the Hebrew Prophet Moses, teaches that the way to atonement with God and Humanity is via heartfelt confession of wrong doing and making amends/reparations and/or restorations, even adding 20% of principal on original offense. But who cares when the devil is in charge? Supreme messages go on deaf ears.

In Leviticus (Lev 6:1-7), we are taught that reparations are a generational responsibility. God will hold one generation responsible and accountable for the wrong doing of previous generations. Humanity may forget the past sins of their ancestors against another people, but God does not. It is only after confession of wrong doing followed by reparations, is the forgiveness granted and atonement finished.

Christ, in Matthew 5 23-26, teaches that without reparations, God will not hear prayer nor receive praise and thanksgiving.

Filled with hope and faith, Africans, like others in their group, clearly understand Jeremiah's teaching (Jer 32:17) – 'Ah, sovereign Lord, you

          Needless Suffering

have made the heavens and the earth by your great power. Nothing is too hard for you'. This, in apparent reference to the awesome power of the creator who can change the status quo that we find ourselves subjected to.

Why Satan is so brutal, deceiving and cunning, no one knows the answer for sure. Instead of embracing civilization and using it to help indigenous people and build relationships for the good of mankind, armed colonialists maimed, killed and robbed the indigenous people of their asserts and resources.

Today, in-spite of the immense contribution that slavery and colonialism brought to western countries, no single western country is prepared to say sorry and move on wholeheartedly to plough back to Africa and other formerly colonised regions. When they invest in Africa, they expect harvesting returns per dollar of investment ten times more than they make in their own countries. Of course, this has negative consequences to local countries' economies.

Why? Simply, because of the heinous nature of the system. I blame Satan for this. If colonialists had joined hands with natives, to build roads, hospitals, schools airports etc. in good faith, we wouldn't have seen such suffering and struggles of the colonised to free themselves. On the contrary, schools were built so that the masters could communicate easily with labourers. Equally, hospitals were set up so that the source of labour would be fit to work. Of all the 55 African countries, only one - Ethiopia - was never colonized but suffered immeasurably from temporary Italian occupation. All others had to fight to be free, one way or another.

The video (End of an Empire [1985]), chapter 14: Rhodesia) - https://www.youtube.com/watch?v=0DuNhsLR9y0) depicts how man and women risked their lives by throwing themselves off the cliff in order to free their countries from the yoke of colonialism and how the privileged colonialists fought tooth and nail to defend their ill-gotten wealth, but to no avail.

Also, the amazing sacrificial effort shown in: 'Zimbabwe's Liberation - a short and accurate history', tells it all.

Quite often people say the over exploitation of resources by former colonial powers such as Great Britain, France, Spain, Belgium and Germany among others, left Africa and former colonies from other regions poorer. The exploits were shipped to the colonial masters' motherlands for the development of their countries. It's a case of building one's nest with others' feathers. The harsh forms of colonialism, where the masters abused the natives and paid no regard to their right to enjoy the resources of their countries, equally caused a discrepancy in wealth distribution.

In most cases, natives were excluded from wealth creation activities. For example, they had very few opportunities of setting up businesses as they had no access to capital, land and institutional support. Much of the fertile land was taken away by the colonialists and the little that wasn't was commercialized beyond the reach of natives. Those who were pushed to the marginal areas bore the brand of sharing their produce with baboons, pigs and other wild animals; thanks to the immoral nature of mankind.

Besides all this, Apartheid, a systemic form of racial segregation was enacted and enforced through legislation by South Africa's National Party against the natives. It was severest in SA and less so in other countries like Rhodesia, Mozambique Angola and many others. Choice of job, school, hospital, beer-hall and what house to build and where was based on racial segregation principles. Needless to delve any deeper into apartheid stories, suffice to say that every adult of our time clearly recognizes this heinous system which was premised on the evil principles of Eugenics.

A form of Apartheid system existed in most colonised African countries for many years. Needlessly, thousands of human lives were lost. The brutality of colonialism is revealed by honest and repentant descendants of colonialists (https:// youtu.be/wkrkfaUMAxQ). Unfortunately, it comes late and doesn't go far enough to encourage any form of restoration. They confirm that colonialism was brutal, cruel and evil.

Consider the untold suffering African tribes in India (Sidis, Jawaras etc.), who were dumped there by colonialist during slave trade era. The Jawaras face extinction.

They live like wild animals (https://www.survivalinternational.org/tribes/jarawa). Surely, they should be compensated by the culprit former colonizing countries, for the sake of justice and morality.

In South Africa, Apartheid was promulgated into law in 1948 but ended by 1994 following the release of Nelson Mandela from the notorious Robben Island prison.

Stories of liberation of Algeria, Zimbabwe, Angola, Mozambique and other African countries are nerve-racking. Futile attempts by former colonial masters to reverse independence by creating and supporting counter revolutionaries like Dr Savimbi's UNITA in Angola and 'Matsanga's Renamo rebel movement in Mozambique are heart-rending when you consider the devastation, they caused during post liberation period. Colonialism had similar effect in the Indian subcontinent and Latin America.

Resources such as iron ore, cobalt zinc, gold etc., were extracted at very low prices and shipped abroad for processing into finished goods such as cars, computers etc., and then sold back to developing countries from which raw materials came, at very high prices. Interestingly, this can appear justified as the multinational companies talk of employment creation and Direct Foreign Investment (FDIs) coming to these poor countries. But, suppose 'fiat money' (currency without intrinsic value) is used in FDIs in Africa or any other region, would this not translate into predatory exploitation, something akin to extorting critical assets and strategic resources of these countries.

In an award-winning documentary film – 'The Four Horsemen' - Ross Ashcroft, writer and director, narrates a harrowing story of our time - the Age of Consequences - in which he reveals how the world really works. The consequences referred to arise from the stupid system man created. It is a system that has been built by barbaric, greedy and corrupt leaders who steal or pay themselves hefty salaries while billions of people face unspeakable hardships from a system whose laws favour the interests of a few people.

I have traversed diverse countries such as USA, Belgium, Ireland, Tanzania, Kenya, SA, Zimbabwe and UK, and have seen with my eyes the misery that is afflicting millions of ordinary people. The system is characterized by obscene levels of immorality and decadence which have become the norm, resulting in escalating organized crime, looming environmental fallout, wars and deaths of innocent people across the world.

In 'The Four Horsemen', Ross and his colleagues explicitly reveal the reason why many people now are in a state of confusion, not understanding how they got into this ugly vicious cycle of hardships. The 'Four Horsemen' represents views of ordinary people as told by great men of valor, the likes of Noam Chomsky, Marx Keizer and others, who stand to speak the truth in the face of collective delusion. They show how gatekeepers have manipulated the human cognitive mind. Imagine in this 21st century having bank leaders who award themselves severance packages including bonuses worth millions at a time when their banks go bankrupt – causing serious hardships to ordinary people. Such was the case following the 2008 global financial meltdown that affected millions of people, mostly the poor.

It has been revealed that behind the turmoil sit very immoral, camouflaged people, who appear to be telling the truth and yet all they do is to hoodwink people into thinking that all is well while they drive everyone to the cliff edge.

Among other factors, the 'Four Horsemen' blames mankind's immorality and greed that has led to the establishment of neo-classical economic order (predatory capitalism) which cares less for the ordinary people.

 Needless Suffering

Predatory capitalism preaches free market economics with minimal regulation. But the opposite is what we see - low wage labour, mushrooming of tax havens, inadequate or bogus social systems and deprivation of the people. Inept governments and multinational corporations project the picture that, when they amass large amounts of capital and wealth, that wealth will trickle-down to the ordinary workers and society at large. But the reality is that only a tiny fraction of such wealth goes to the people and even then, only a portion of that wealth does so as such money quickly loose value. All the while, the wealthy corporates stashes billions of dollars in off-show accounts.

The western world is thought to have toppled the original Adam Smith's Classical Economic model – (The Theory of Moral Sentiments (1759)'. It's a fantastic model that influenced the likes of Karl Max, Thomas Malthus, Anne Robert Jacques and others who went on to produce great works that helped shape our modern world in the spheres of politics and economics. This model advocates capitalistic market development, more personal autonomy and recognising that humans need resources to function well and that wealth should be distributed equitably.

It boggles the mind to see that, instead of promoting noble economic models, the highly educated peoples of the world, led by highly immoral leaders, have soiled Classical Economics as a true model for economic emancipation and replaced it by a vicious neoclassical economic model. Surely, proponents of capitalism, in pursuit of profit, sees no moral boundaries.

Neo-classical economics is blamed for denying people their socio-cultural and economic needs. Under this system, multi-national corporations blossom while inequality gaps widen by the day and poverty creeps into people's homes.

The neocons are good at working hand-in-glove with kleptocratic governments especially of Africa. In pursuit of profit, they have (corporations) legitimized the financialization of the global economy, which they control in their favour.

Some western governments have exported misery and injustice through debt finance to unsuspecting or undemocratic governments who pass these debts to their citizens. Despite abundance of resources, this system has caused havoc, ruining lives of billions and caused destructive global conflicts.

When they get to Africa, they use cheap 'fiat money' for investments-FDIs. They target profit margins ranging from 50% to 100%+, whereas in the western world they can only be assured of under 20% in most of their investments. What would happen if Africa could borrow such cheap money at, say, 2% and lends it to its citizens to kick start projects leaving out FDIs to focus only

 Needless Suffering

on complex projects.? Certainly, this is the way to go but alas, certain forces make it impossible.

In most sectors, FDIs are encouraged by inept governments to spread their tentacles across all economic sectors leaving citizens to serve as consumers and powerless workers. This is a painful reality of the consequences of immorality. Just visualize a situation where fiat money is used to buy large quantities of gold, zinc, nickel copper etc. in poor countries. Obviously key resources from these countries will be taken almost for free. Meanwhile, such countries into which the gold goes, base their currencies on the strength of the gold reserves they possess making such currency very powerful – capable of purchasing anything from anywhere on earth.

Western governments benefits from high corporate taxes while their citizens enjoy jobs which their vibrant industries create, courtesy of the power of predatory capitalism. African leaders continue to receive handsome bribes by these corporations who seek favours to exploit resources.

Think of what is happening in Congo (DRC). My heart bleeds - and bleeds heavily in deed! Various news outlets reported biggest electoral fraud in recent history, where the winning opposition leader was sidelined and a stooge was picked up by the loosing incumbent to take over. This is the scale of corruption in Africa. All this for the sake of sustaining corrupt officials' pot bellies at the expense of the suffering masses.

Amazingly, though, the Grace of God is upon us. The birth of the internet has brought about hope that we can transform our lives. It brought about enlightenment and has, according to Ross, removed the cloud of ignorance upheld by academics and media gatekeepers. The end of mass mind-control is nigh. We are now able to see with our eyes and understand the ugly nature of the human mind. It gets darker before dawn.

Endurance leads to glorious results. Hebrews 11:1 teaches us: "Faith is being sure of what we hope for and certain of what we do not see". We are hopeful and certain that change will come, at least in our life time. Think about it: great powers like the United Kingdom is leading in championing change - from slave trader champion and <u>super imperial power</u> to becoming anti-slavery and Equality and Diversity champion, at a global scale. This is bringing relief and sanity to the planet we all love, although much more is expected.

The creation of the <u>Africa Free Trade area</u> is probably a game changer in our life time as this will unlock Africa's enormous potential. No one can really comprehend the scale, but what I know for certain is that more than 60% of rich fertile agricultural land is found in Africa; much of the critical mineral resources needed for our modern *lives such as gold, oil and those for making electric cars or mobile smart phones resides in Africa in abundance; this continent has a fair share of best sunshine on earth, fresh water and the associated fauna and flora - vegetation and wildlife is abundant, in fact, this is unparalleled by any other continent. Just visualize the Maasai Mara, Kruger or Manna pools wildlife sanctuaries - true wonders of the Lord's creation. More than 60% of its people are energetic youths gifted with intellect and are well educated and in some countries represents highly skilled manpower – all waiting for the dawn of a new Africa.*

I submit to you my brethren and sisters, the brutal system ruling us will eventually fall and the lives of the oppressed and the poor will be changed for the better. What then do we ought to do to restructure our socio-economic system? Among many factors, reforming taxation systems in order to refloat poor countries' economies; enacting laws that levels up the playing field for all business; promoting democratic governments through restructured political systems and embracing unadulterated Classical Economic principles.

Ross Ashcroft, Max Keizer, Noam Chomsky and others, call upon all ordinary people to be responsible and take action in restructuring the ugly system mankind has created. This is possible if people can be encouraged to read, learn and understand the circumstance of our time; to walk with eyes wide open so as to avoid pitfalls and never to miss an opportunity – for the sake of future generations.

In my opinion, this is the time when we need to ask our governments to usher in affirmative action and allow ordinary citizens to regain their lives though 'Affirmative Community Commonwealth development projects'. 'Community' refers to people or groups of ordinary people who come together to join hands in raising seed capital to start and run scalable business projects.

At national, regional or global level, this approach can produce phenomenal results. Given the global Afro-diaspora phenomenon, once adopted, it will be easy to see emergence of mega projects in, say, mining, retail malls, AI, manufacturing, agribusiness, infrastructure development and many more areas. Imagine the poor local natives (who get government affirmative support) and just half of hundreds of thousands of successful diaspora Africans teaming up to set-up the 'Silicon Valley projects' of Kinshasa or Brasilia, or setting-up high-tech meat processing factories in Addis Ababa for Arab market or exploiting gas fields of Mozambique or Zimbabwe. It's possible. We will not only catch-up but overtake the developed countries, while in the process ending poverty and needless suffering that has been imposed on the poor.

I salute the ordinary peoples of Europe particularly of Great Britain for standing by the side of the poor peoples of the world, during times of trouble. Ordinary Britons have always, since time immemorial, walked into the streets to demonstrate in solidarity with the oppressed people, for example during Apartheid and colonialism in general. Such gallant acts changed the course of history although much more still has to be done in light of the rise of predatory capitalism.

More than ever before, we need a model form of capitalism to propel the global economy forward. Currently our greatest enemy is predatory capitalism.

I have always wondered whether it is a case of our Lord conspiring against his people. Why should abject poverty continue to haunt billions of people? As already noticed, fingers point to the broken financial system at the heart of predatory capitalism.

Martha Leah Nangala describes plunder of Congo's resources by the Western World, as the silent holocaust. The documentary, 'Friends of the Congo' (https://congojustice.org/), uncovers the whole truth. It spins nerves down the spine; heart rending in deed. In the process of the plunder, those involved do not care about the native people. They kill or sponsor killings as they push for resource exploitation. Since 1996 the Democratic Republic of Congo (DRC) has lost more than six million people through conflicts sponsored by exploiters.

It would appear neither the UN nor the AU or any other global organisation has any constructive voice over what is happening in DRC, some commentators would say. This is a shameful tragedy of our time. Ironically, the civilized world-the so-called developed world- appear unmoved by this tragedy. Why is the world journalistic community silent about this? Where are the powerful western media organisations? You may wonder.

Paradoxically, with the exception of tiny minority, the native poor are denied a chance to make any meaningful investment in their own countries nor in the western markets as they don't have the capital, skills and resources to get involved.

Poor peoples of the world need to be empowered first so they can embark and participate in economic development of their countries. Once economically empowered, they can buy stakes in all economic sectors.

Lost Opportunities

If the western world had abandoned Neo-Classical Economic Model and embraced Classical Models, much could have been achieved in Africa and the whole world. People would bring up novel

 Needless Suffering

innovations leading to production of goods and services that are desperately needed to support life.

We could be talking of getting support from business angels, joint ventures/equity finance and business incubation schemes. A win-win situation could prevail and all of humanity would be guaranteed of prosperity. But this is just as good as a pipe dream for now. More work needs to be done.

Because of the intrinsic nature of predatory capitalism, much has been lost – material resources, financial capital and life itself - to mention but a few of the negative effects of an immoral system. Remodeling this bad system is the greatest challenge of our time. We have no choice, everyone has to participate in reversing the status quo, for the sake of our children.

Ordinary citizens have spilled the beans. They have told shocking stories of how the western powers accepts a few blacks into their countries when they see a benefit in doing so, but are quick to get rid of them when they don't see any benefit.

They remark on how missionaries were used to preach the Gospel of Christ to win minds of unsuspecting Africans. Quite often, fuzzy concepts are used to confuse the poor nations, which allows predator nations to siphon resources without being scrutinised. These ordinary Euro-citizens will tell you that, the west is like a lion that survives on preying on other animals. Africa and any other unsuspecting regions are the prey.

Other nations, especially some East European and Asian countries, are described as having quickly understood the west's game play and have developed counter measures to exploitation, which Africans have failed to do.

Telling it as it is, indeed! The plain truth. Yes, Africans do have weaknesses as have been explained in earlier sections on African greed, but to a greater extent, it is the deliberate mechanisations of the west that has kept Africans under relentless siege. This represents loss of great opportunities, as far greater things would be achieved if the west worked in partnership with Africa instead of subduing it.

Regardless, some would say the serious problems we face today can be traced back to the birth of the Mercantile System (MS) which took root in Europe in the 1500s. This was a system which fused together ancient and pre-medieval business and economic development philosophies resulting in somewhat a model approach in international business practice. Nonetheless, before long, instead of being an embodiment of modern capitalism, it would soon be highjacked by governments which teamed up with business tycoons and set-up a vehicle for the worst inhuman acts on earth.

The Mercantile System was influenced by extreme desire for wealth creation. The system allowed powerful nations to promote their exports while squeezing weaker countries by levying stringent tariffs on imports from these countries. Pursued properly, the mercantile system went on to produce, even today, some of the best capitalist practices of our time. Modified to include a social component as has been the case in Scandinavian countries, it became somewhat the best socio-capitalist model of our time, with awesome results seen in the development trajectories of these countries. However, excessive desire for money paved the way for slavery by some heartless western countries. Slaves were traded in America and Europe in the same way livestock are traded and all this was to boost business on farms and mines using free labour.

Ideally, mercantilism could easily get credit for giving rise to advanced business systems we have today (e.g. Economics, Business Management, Accountancy and Finance), but unfortunately all accumulated knowledge in these fields is being adulterated due to greed and immorality, and hence the emergence of predatory capitalism. The same mercantile spirit propelled European settlers to commit heinous crimes in the Americas also. The brutal and chaotic scenes in which native Americans were slaughtered or displaced during occupation days leaves a lot to be desired.

Fortunately, historians have made full accounts of these atrocities covering Mexico, Brazil, Chile, Bolivia, Peru, Cuba etc. The list is a long one. While wisdom favours zero retribution, the expectation is that the perpetrators make sincere apologies to the natives of these countries. Let's recall from Leviticus (Lev 6:1-7), that - reparations are a generational responsibility.

Immoral European governments sponsored slave trade merchants during African slavery era and when colonialism became the new norm, they would team up with industry in pursuit of resource exploitation from colonies of such vital minerals as gold, silver and others. Quite often these western governments wouldn't mind about governance of colonies which they left out to administrative units who yielded considerable power, and hence the abuse of natives in colonies which we have all come to understand so well.

While promotion of manufacturing and the evolution of the capitalist spirit would have been the greatest achievement of the mercantile system, it quickly became synonymous with the expansion of colonies overseas (quite often by brutal means) and increased government regulation of trade (often leading to unfair trade practices with weaker countries especially those of Africa). Perhaps no wonder why we now have this vicious form of predatory capitalism around us today.

Mercantilism still influence global trade and geo-politics in modern society. No wonder tariffs and free-trade or the so-called Irish back-stop issue became the Brexit sticking point during negotiations. Perhaps that's why African goods and those from other regions continue to suffer from entry barriers into Europe to this day - and yet European goods literary freely find access into other regions, thus creating a huge trade imbalance and unequitable global trade system leading to negative impacts on ordinary citizens.

Contemporaries argue that the European citizens, whose governments participated in slavery and colonialism, are innocent of the scourges of these twin evils. Invariably, however, they were beneficiaries of the ill-gotten wealth which is still happening today. By nature, European ordinary citizens are very civil and even those who carried out cruel and vicious acts such as <u>throwing of slaves into the sea, during abolition times</u>, did so under duress as they simply carried out orders of their merchant masters.

Historians put the death toll of African lives lost due to slave trade at 14-100ml. Majority died due to savagery and brutality of their enslavers while some, due to apathy, met their fate by throwing themselves into the sea. Pathetic and grim were cases of manslaughter such as the Zong massacre, perpetrated by a Liverpool based Gregson slave-trading syndicate, in which more than 130 African slaves were thrown into the sea so that the slave traders could claim insurance compensation (https://en.wikipedia.org/wiki/Zong_massacre).

In ordinary conversations in Europe one can hear citizens argue over why, it would appear, the elites who went to private schools such as Eton and others - and moved on to such prestigious universities as Cambridge, Oxford and others, do influence the lives of the majority in the UK. There are serious forces behind it. Such people from rich backgrounds live wild and luxurious life styles and lack the empathy necessary to feel for the poor majority. Quite often it's observed across the globe that these are the progeny of oligarchs, business tycoons and despots and their cronies. Today it's not uncommon to hear leaders of the western world supporting despots in elections of foreign countries. You would hear them say, 'Give him a chance', referring to a despot belonging to a kleptocracy – who would be contesting in an election, because under such a system they can afford to siphon resources by bribing-off such barbaric leaders.

Garry Younge, commenting in the Guardian, observed that government and culture were dominated by the same narrow section of population made up of elites who make-up a self-serving clique. Commentators argue that political elites create a system that rewards a privileged minority class, often from wealthy backgrounds. This phenomenon, it is feared, creates crisis after crisis such as the Brexit chaos. (The Guardian - https://www.theguardian.com/commentisfree/2019/jul/05/britain-run-self-serving-clique-crisis-narrow-section).

Perhaps this is the reason why slavery would be allowed to prevail for more than 300 years and colonialism for over 100 years, never mind the Brexit circus to which ordinary Britons have been subjected, of late.

All over the world, the elites control governments and the socio-political sphere. They influence large chunks of critical institutional bodies such as the legal and journalistic fraternity. Where they work hand-in-glove with parastatal and private sector tycoons, check what salaries they get or give to gatekeepers of such systems. Check how bloated salaries of executive gatekeepers in TV/Radio broadcasting parastatals are and also look at the chaos in banks, local authorities etc. It's weird to say the least. It's clear to see why executive gatekeepers of collapsed companies including banks (during financial meltdown times -2008/9) went on to get hefty pecks, regardless. The achievement was simply adding salt to wounds of ordinary citizens.

Amazingly though, through Grace, like millions who went for the ordinary but modest public schools, a few man and women of supreme wisdom and highest levels of intellectual power, and not necessarily from rich family backgrounds, have accessed these elitist institutions. Many of them never succumbed to elitism. They were steadfast in their beliefs and did cling to their cultural heritage and wisdom. Such are the great minds who have gone on to make contributions that changed the course of history in multiple fields – Government, Sociology, Science and Engineering - to name but a few.

From humble backgrounds we find great people inventing such remarkable items like the TV, radio, ships, planes - pioneered by self-educated brothers – the Wright brothers, the 21ˢᵗ century Wi-Fi and many more. Many stood up against predation and for Human Rights and sacrificed their lives to end slavery, colonialism and despotic governments across the globe.

Think of the Theoretical Physicist Stephen Hawking and many others' contributions. The theoretical notion that artificial intelligence (AI), through – for example - gene sequencing science - can prolong life by eliminating impaired or disease-causing genes or eliminating the genes associated with ageing, is so profound.

The development of models that mimic the possibility of humans being able to produce more than enough food by employing state-of-the-art technologies in agricultural food production, is just awesome. Other advances might make it possible for humans to live peacefully without even having to work, simply by using AI. Advancement in Sociology and other social sciences can help humans appreciate life better and respect one another in a more humane way, which can enhance peace on earth. Conversely, AI can lead to man's extinction. Civilization, especially when pioneered by forces aligned to predatory capitalists and driven by excessive desire for wealth, can easily be the catalyst in bringing forward the demise of mankind. This is more so when AI is misapplied. Social norms will change and system of values will be altered, all causing great danger to the survival of man. These are the sort of contemporary issues that we should be focusing on in our time and I wonder if ever anything else can take precedence.

Contemporary critiques would argue why, despite the evil nature of slavery and popular demand for its abolition, western governments still would thwart these popular demands.

When outsmarted, predatory capitalism can put up a vicious fight such as sparking senseless trade wars that can throw global economies into a tailspin, with gruesome humanitarian consequences. The elites in government would and still continue to appear to legislate in favour of the masses but in actual fact this is only window dressing for political expediency. My friend Peter sought answers: 'Since time immemorial, did the political elites hold ordinary people to ramson'. Mary from Halifax yelled, 'Oooh yes, it's all in the open — the Sutton Trust Report tells it all (https://www.suttontrust.com/research-paper/elitist-britain-2019/). Social mobility is in trouble and the social strata is characterized by poverty-stricken majority who are controlled by a super-rich minority. It has become increasingly common knowledge that the enemy of the masses of the world are not only despots and oligarchs but also the elites and the predatory capitalist system which they selfishly sustain for their own survival.

<u>The Windrush scandal</u> shows the colour of the elites' minds in British politics. Despite being born British and descendants of the forebearer Windrush generation of the 70s, who came to prop-up British industries by providing essential services such as bus driving, nursing, cleaning etc., they (some) were forcibly and wrongly deported. For all this, perhaps because their services were no longer needed, at least in the elites' minds — never mind the afflicted had a life to live.

At the height of the scandal, majority were denied legal recourse. Some lost jobs and others lost homes - whole livelihoods. Such is the colour of the minds of global elites. It took man and women of valour in the legislature to reverse the diabolic decision and to arrange compensation for the afflicted. No wonder why ordinary immigrants face untold hardships in their quest to integrate into European countries. And yet in Africa and perhaps elsewhere, immigrant Europeans are treated as special guests with special rights in society, the workplace and institutionally. While it is immoral for Africans to revenge, they expect reciprocity from their European counterparts. Alas! Our friends appear over-occupied for anything sensible like that.

The good leaders of Europe, however, like John Wesley, Wilberforce or Elizabeth in the slavery abolition struggle, continue to fight for the rights of the asylum seekers, immigrants and the down-trodden citizens. This is particularly true for Britain and some EU countries. Plausible indeed! It's heart-rending, though, to observe that ordinary EU citizens are not aware of the sacrifices of millions of African slaves, whose blood and sweat watered the bedrock of modern western industrial economies. They simply focus on enjoying the benefits.

The failings of man are further shown by the circus-like Brexit jigsaw puzzle, which took over two years to resolve. This sheds light on why the <u>*heinous slavery trade*</u> *took three hundred years to abolish. Across the globe, political elites are called hawks in apparent likeness to the birds of prey that mercilessly pounce on unsuspecting animals for food. But surely, do humans have to pride themselves in behaving like hawks?*

I asked a British friend why the Brexit project took such an arduous path that was characterized by confusion and consternation of the citizens. He said, 'It's obvious, when people are not made aware of the truth, they are bound to make wrong decisions. In the Brexit Referendum, people simply 'voted with their stomachs' and not on solid facts. Majority of the electorate did not fully understand the socio-economic benefits of being part of the Euro-project, which in a way is huge.

One in the neighborhoods could be heard chanting, 'Peddlers of lies easily preyed upon people's ignorance by churning out falsehoods, and hence the Brexit fiasco'. It became a conundrum as democracy means respecting the people's will and the Brexiteers had to be respected. But democracy works when it is participatory in nature and when people are knowledgeable. And yet, in most countries, institutions and citizens are ill-informed and do not play any meaningful role in the politics and governance of their countries. Resultantly, they make irrational political decisions. Ironically, African despots - who in the past distorted and abused the famous Marxist principles - are now copying the western trait of ruling by sustaining ignorance of the electorate, who blindly vote for the opposite of what is good for them.

     Needless Suffering

A lot of international observers are dumbfounded as to why Trump would win in USA against all odds and why brilliant brains in the likes of Hammond in the British Conservative Party would not make any move for the vacant premiership post following May's departure. Instead, at a crucial moment in time, Boris led the pack.

The case of immorality, injustice and pursuit of wealth through predatory means was made by one luminary African Union Ambassador to the USA, H.E Dr Arikana Chihombori Quao, while addressing the African diaspora in the Americas - (https://www.youtube.com/watch?v=aXMP1Az5HL8&feature=youtu.be). Dr Arikana fearlessly reveals the dark side of the human mind by explicitly narrating the account of the Berlin Conference of 1884-85 (The General Act of the Berlin Conference), where Africa and its resources were determined by the western powers.

Initiated by Portugal and organized by Otto von Bismarck, first Chancellor of Germany, the General Act of the Berlin Conference, culminated into the formalization of the Scramble for Africa. Subsequently, European powers increased their grip on colonies while simultaneously eliminating most existing forms of African autonomy and self-governance. Today, the notorious anti-Africa resolutions still hold sway.

Shame! Many Pan-Africanists believe the scramble for Africa's resources formed the foundations of predatory capitalism. Colonialists stopped at nothing as they murdered African leaders in order to gain free access to resources. For example, as they resisted colonialism, Zimbabwean African leaders - Nehanda Nyakasikana and Kaguvi Gumboreshumba, of Mashonaland - were captured and executed in 1898 by settler colonialist agents. The Christmas tree became a shrine in Zimbabwe, in honour of those who perished for resisting colonialism. Their sacrifices inspired the liberation struggle which brought an end to the brutal colonial system.

It all started in the 15th and 16th centuries when Portugal and Spain pioneered the European exploration of the globe. In the process they acquired large overseas empires, in Asia and the Americas. This was the start of colonialism. England, France and The Netherlands followed suit by setting up their own colonies and trade networks in North America and Asia. Great Britain, as it was then called after its conquest of Scotland in 1707 would soon set up an empire comprising dominions, colonies, protectorates, and other territories she ruled.

At its peak by 1923, the British Empire ruled over 412ml people, 23% of the global population. By 1920 it had occupied 35.5ml km2, that's 24% of the earth's total land mass. By far the British

Empire had the most widespread legacy in terms of legal, cultural, linguistic and political influence. The British East India Company helped Britain dominate the Indian Sub-continent. The years 1815-1914 were described as the period of the British hegemony during which it adopted role of global policeman. Wealth from colonialism helped it prop-up its industries leading to unparalleled economic might from the Industrial Revolution.

In his book, The Scramble for Africa (1876 to 1912), Thomas Pakenham describes how European Powers savagely occupied and colonised Africa. Several brutal wars which characterized European conquest of Africa were fought against unsuspecting but peace-loving African natives. https://en.wikipedia.org/wiki/The_Scramble_ for_Africa_(book).

By 1870, 10% of Africa was snatched away and by end of 1914, 90% was gone except Ethiopia which remained independent.

The British South Africa Company (BSAC), formed after the merger between Cecil John Rhodes' Central Search Association and the London-based Exploring Company Ltd, was set up with the backing of the British government with the objective of economic exploitation across much of South-Central Africa, as part of the Scramble of Africa. The BSAC received British Royal Charter in 1889 just like the British East

India Company which helped Britain in colonizing India sub-continent.

It is advisable, though, to great leaders like H.E Dr Arikana to consider that any move towards freeing Africa from the grip of dictatorships and neo-capitalism, should start with setting up of an independent Pan-African electoral body that freely and independently organises and runs elections in Africa, especially for rogue states.

We have seen electoral chaos across Africa as if these were sponsored by a 'hidden hand' to discredit native Africans and allow for unfettered resource exploitation. The electoral quarrels in DRC, Congo, Kenya, Zimbabwe and others are exemplary cases. If proper elections were run in these countries, truly democratic governments - with international recognition and support - could have been created and hence unlocking the enormous potential of Africa.

It is now common knowledge that superpowers are again scrambling for control and exploitation of Africa's resources such as, among many, cobalt, zinc, lithium, gold, nickel, uranium and tantalum from coltan which is used to manufacture batteries for electric cars and electronic products including mobile phones. Imagine western powers joining hands with African countries to exploit these resources on a win-win mutual basis; how much progress would be achieved? And yet the status quo is a predatory scenario associated with brutal wars that's causing so much havoc and hindering Africa from moving forward. True, the 'new scramble for African resources' largely excludes Africans.

A ground-breaking research by Mark Curtis [July 2016], for a charity (War on Want), which fights against the root causes of poverty and human rights violations as part of a world-wide movement for global justice, revealed that Africa is today facing 'a new colonial invasion' no less than that which it suffered during the nineteenth century (https://waronwant. org/sites/default/files/TheNewColonialism. pdf?_ga=2.74525270.550216632.1554658194-881801983.1554658194).

Mark observes that the London Stock Exchange has been dominated by 101 companies, mostly British. These entities control over $1trillion worth of Africa's resources in just five commodities – oil, gold, diamonds, coal and platinum. This behavior is akin to a new 'Scramble for Africa' that is proceeding apace.

As has been observed by other researchers mentioned earlier, Mark's research has revealed that, while FDIs are a necessity, not all of them serve the needs of host countries. On the contrary and in a majority of cases, they are set-up to illicitly exploit resources of these poor countries.

The fear, now then, is that African governments have probably handed over their treasure, in light of the fact that these western companies have acquired mineral licenses in 37 Sub-Saharan African countries and control vast swathes of land in excess of 1million square km. These multinational firms are extracting Zambia's Copper, South Africa's platinum, Tanzania's gold, Botswana's diamonds – the list goes on and on.

Shamefully, western liberal free trade and investment policies that preclude African governments from setting up counter regulatory or protectionist barriers to foreign investments, have been promulgated. Perplexingly, the western governments backed by their super-rich corporate firms appear devoid of any Christian mercy. How come they can't help the thousands of Africans drowning in the Mediterranean Sea when they are gaining vastly from Africa and other Emerging Markets.

It's as if Hitler's Eugenics principles are still at play in this 21ˢᵗ century. Governments, through rigorous and robust policies do fight these racial vices but loopholes still do exist. A lot of great managers in UK, France, Germany and elsewhere work hard to complement their governments in fighting racial segregation, but quite often they are overwhelmed by the moribund performance of their peers, who hamper such efforts due to their retrogressive behaviour. Afro-diaspora citizens have seen it all. They, like everyone else, equally blame barbaric and greedy African leaders who have allowed their citizens to bear the brunt of European racial discrimination, vilification and inhuman condescending treatment.

Back to empirical research findings: Unlike Africa, East Asia and other regions have been able to counter some neoliberal policies which are responsible for producing such bad systems.

In Africa, western governments have promoted and advocated low corporate taxes thus allowing their companies to get away with huge profits which they stash in off-shore safe heavens.

Mark concludes by lamenting that the result of Africa's illicit resource exploitation by the west has made Africa, the world's poorest continent.

Mark advocates a radical rethink on the notion that the west is helping Africa to develop. Large western aid programmes are used to promote policies that allow western corporations to enjoy hefty profit.

A compassionate call is upon the UK public to engage in solidarity actions in the UK to hold British companies and the British government accountable.

The empathetic ordinary British citizens, owing to their high level of civilization and a fighting spirit for morality and justice - if properly persuaded – can act and change the status quo as they have done during days of the heinous Apartheid system of South Africa. In their millions, they have braved chilling temperatures to demonstrate in the streets of London, Manchester, Hull, Birmingham and elsewhere against injustice unfolding on our planet.

In the final analysis, we can easily see that there is need for a radical shift in the way we view and deal with donors and foreign governments and their corporations who masquerade as champions in FDIs for Africa and other regions.

This is true if Africa, like the rest of the world, is to achieve serious and sustainable development that ensures long term economic development. The unsuspecting, poorly educated and misinformed Africans, like those ones in the same group the world over, stand no chance to predatory capitalism. In western countries, the education system precludes passing on of truthful historical accounts on the origins of predatory capitalism, contribution of slavery to development of western countries, why Africa remains subdued and poor as it is and why this is allowed to continue unchallenged.

By answering these questions, it is hoped man can acquire true knowledge and hence forth free themselves from ignorance and perhaps get the urge to act and make our world a better place to live. And here-in lies the prudent idea of Affirmative Community Commonwealth

Movement that should replace or completement FDIs for the benefit of native citizens.

If the world can benefit so hugely from a rising China, as an example, how about global economic contribution of a rising Africa? Immeasurable benefits can be reaped indeed. Don't we need more of DRC's mobile cell-phone minerals? You can answer yourself. But do we need to get these minerals by hook and crook – sponsoring the mayhem we see today in DRC or Africa at large.

History always repeats itself. Countless empires came and sunk into oblivion. The British Empire, the Roman Empire, Ottoman Empire, Mongols, Russian Empire, Spanish Empire, Qing dynasty, Ming dynasty and several others are all gone - and gone for ever. Astonishingly, in spite of this phenomenal knowledge which mankind have, we still find ourselves failing to embrace the morality doctrine for our survival.

Contribution of Slavery to Poverty

Slavery stands out as one of the earliest causes of untold suffering and poverty in Africa.

Historical accounts talk of Asian slavery and European ancient slavery that was practiced by rich Feudal Lords over the poor where the rich simply dragged the poor for unpaid labour.

However, by far the gravest of all evils was African slavery in the last three hundred years or so – from 1441 to late 19ᵗʰ century. Besides causing despicable suffering to the enslaved, who were treated like wild animals, the slave masters exploited the slaves' blood, using them for monetary gain. Slaves were traded and sold in auctions like animals. In source countries it meant entire families were wiped off. Those who remained had no one to fend for them. Slave labour to their masters in America and Europe was immense.

In Europe and America, slavery contributed trillions of dollars to the fiscus. Both America and Britain paid reparations to slave owners—not to slaves or those countries which incurred human and economic losses due to slavery. Slavery launched modern western capitalism, turning U.S. into the wealthiest country in the world.

Inversely, slavery depleted Africa of its material resources and human capital, causing immeasurable human suffering.

Poverty in Africa and the warped reasoning characteristics of some African leaders can be traced to the effects of slavery. Trauma and psychological impairment which slavery brought on the minds of Africans and their leaders were horrendous. Imagine majority of the African kings were forced, by threat of gunpower, to capture their subjects i.e. children, men and women into

     Needless Suffering

slavery for the slave master. This seems to have had the greatest enduring negative influence in the mindset of Africans. In today's terms, all survivors of slavery could be put through years of post-traumatic disorder therapy so they could regain some semblance of normalcy, and yet nothing of the sort ever happened.

The greatest debate of our time is to try and understand if Africans could have behaved the same way as the Europeans did against them if they had developed the gun earlier than other races. What's your take?

Great history tellers have given serious highlights on some fundamental facts about African slavery. Before 1400, classical slavery had existed in Europe and did not disappear when the Roman Empire collapsed around 476AD, according to historian Edward Gibbon.

With the advent of increased trade across the Mediterranean and the Atlantic seaboard, African slaves began to appear in Italy, Spain, Southern France, and Portugal well before the discovery of the New World in 1492.

Initially, Portuguese captains Antão Gonçalves and Nuno Tristão captured 12 Africans in Cabo Branco (modern Mauritania) and took them to Portugal as slaves and thus sparking the start of European slave trading in Africa, in 1441.

Probably the reason why slavery was ever born is due to the ugly mind of mankind. Much is revealed in the video - 'Hegemony'- depicting Christopher Columbus and the genocidal activities that engulfed the Americas - forerunner to the slave trade. Check it out on https://youtu.be/ NntSplMam7Q. This is also revealed in 'Crimes against humanity – African slavery', which reveals the true social impact of injustice and immorality.

From Africa's political view point, slavery and colonialism have been the commonest drivers of poverty. The invention of the gun by the western world is somewhat to blame. It was used to heinously force African leaders to abduct their citizens and hand them over to enslavers.

The Nature of African Greed

Just as it were during colonial days, in post-independence era, many African leaders have taken away or denied citizens freedoms and access to natural resources, due to greed. This has been due to relentless pursuit of power by these ass-licking, greedy demagogues. They preside over obscenely profligate and callous regimes. Their actions have caused untold poverty and suffering across the continent (https://www.youtube.com/ watch?v=iw7mDNTmFJk).

Even when they see people in dire need of help for financial capital or material inputs to set up any meaningful project, these leaders will continue to squander anything at their disposal – money, state assets or making unnecessary travels across the globe. Any attempts by the citizens to set up projects will be futile due to inadequate capital and absence of supportive pro-people financial services. Skills training centres are non-existent or ill-equipped to support proper skills development. All the while, the leaders are busy amassing wealth for themselves, buying properties abroad and sending their children to expensive private schools at home or abroad. Many are polygamous, to satisfy their insatiable sex appetite.

Some critiques say that poverty in Africa started with slavery, which was succeeded by colonialism and neo-colonialism. Neo-colonialism has been blamed for creating conditions for incessant ineptitude and greed of national leaders. Western powers control these leaders in return for favours (kick-backs) but at the expense of the poor citizens. For example, large swathes of land or lucrative mining concessions are granted to capitalists in the name of FDIs, but all this at the expense of local citizens. It doesn't mean FDIs are not wanted for development, the key thing is to allow FDIs to venture into critical capital-intensive projects, not simple projects which locals can do.

Quite often local communities are whittled out of business or denied any opportunity to start businesses because of the ugly nature of inept governments. Most corrupt governments prefer to give away land and business opportunities to FDIs and oligarchs who give kick-backs to such corrupt officials.

Today, oligarchs, government officials and their cronies team up with FDI corporates to set up business empires in poor countries in the name of wealth and employment creation. However, in most cases this is a mere smokescreen, as majority of the people do not benefit from these investments in any meaningful way. They just get scraps. The cream of the wealth is siphoned-off by these multinationals and their cohorts. It is not uncommon for these corporations to generate more revenue than the host countries because they dodge taxes or simply externalize funds to off-shore accounts.

Because of inert greed, African leaders have set up dictatorships or kleptocratic regimes which guarantees them an opportunity to systematically siphon wealth at the expense of the ordinary people. They create policies and conditions which make it impossible or difficult for ordinary citizens to exploit their talents, let alone nurture these talents to generate wealth for themselves and their children. Opponent party members are persecuted. Today, online resources are loaded with information on 'dictators of Africa'. Horrible! That's the nature of greed in Africa.

Because of such circumstances, a lot of talent is put to waste in Africa. Those talented youths, men and women who would otherwise come up with novel ideas to develop their countries, just die away without realizing their dreams. All the intuitive ideas and innovations which would otherwise change the face of Africa and the entire world, are needlessly lost.

Those who align with the evil systems of kleptocratic governments will set up shop or briefcase firms to syphon the national wealth. They become filthy rich at the expense of the majority. It is the evil leaders who allow this to happen. They consciously support the rise of their friends and relatives as well as cronies. It's all supported by a system of patronage set-up by these barbaric leaders. This rampant system ensures continued suffering of the poor masses. To continue to blame effects of slavery or colonialism is misleading as some of those countries which were once colonies e.g. South Korea have overcome these effects and have moved on to economically overtake many countries which were never colonised.

Another cause for Africa's poverty is directly corelated to debt. Many African countries, soon after attaining freedom and independence from former colonial masters, were coerced into taking up expensive debts, hoodwinked into believing that these debts would bring prosperity to their countries. In most cases these were mere traps to kill the African spirit for survival and renaissance. The greedy African leaders easily got enticed into this because, in the process, they steal large amounts of that debt money. In so doing they reverse the anticipated gains of such loans.

Can the poor people of the world manage to disentangle themselves from the bondage of poverty imposed against them by man-made forces? It's possible. The answer lies in fighting the negative forces of the human mind. Take for instance how governments spend cash for weapons at the expense of their people. A single government can afford to buy $5bl worth of arms where there is no threat of war at all. How many houses could be built for the poor without a roof over their heads with the same amount?

At a minimum cost of $20000 per unit, $5bl can build 250000 housing units for the poor. But governments choose to throw away such large amounts of money into 'sewer drains' just for political expediency, as they buy unnecessary fighter jets and other purposeless military hardware. Government officials get handsome kickbacks when these arms deals are made. A case in point is that of former South African president who was embroiled in corruption scandal in which, allegedly, he accepted bribes from a French arms firm. Billions of dollars were spent on arms instead of financing poverty alleviation *programmes for the crying millions of poor South Africans*

The same money could have, literally speaking, wiped off poverty in SA. While all this happens, corporates rake in huge profits from their businesses of shame. In other African countries as well as other regions, corruption has seen the running down of roads, telecoms, schools, hospitals – pretty much everything that serves peoples' needs and wants. Just consider acts of dictators, the likes of Omar al-Bashir of Sudan who had to be removed by people power from office. Don't forget others like Marcos of Philippines and his wife Imelda who were so corrupt they amassed more than $5b of ill-gotten wealth at the expense of the masses.

Latin America is no exception. Anastasio Somoza of Nicaragua (1896-1956), who, with his family members, savaged his people for fifty years, was a formidable dictator. The same happened in Mexico under dictator Diaz Porfirio (1830-1915) who had to be removed from power through a Mexican revolution.

In Chile, dictator Pinochet (1915-2006) grabbed power by waging a coup that deposed a democratically elected president, Allende Salvador. He went on to preside over a brutal regime which was responsible for thousands of deaths of innocent people.

Amazingly, majority of these dictators had some backing from powerful nations one way or another for geo-political gains.

As noted earlier, some governments even initiate wars which they wage so they can allocate huge budgets for war effort. The ordinary people foot the bills through national taxation system, while government officials and their cronies rake in huge profits from the arms deals directly or indirectly though their shares in such enterprises. This is the evil nature of humankind and is the very reason why we have obscene levels of inequality and poverty in a global village of plenty.

The 2008 financial crisis saw the forces of predatory capitalism influence governments to bail out corporations which they owned. But a fraction of the same mounts could have wiped out hunger on the face of the planet. Alas! It never happens like that. It's shameful that in countries which are or have been tainted by corruption at one point or another, the likes of Brazil, Mexico, Colombia, Nigeria, Zimbabwe, Malawi, South Africa or any other, poverty is rife. One has to be connected to powerful forces to own property or means of production.

People of the world, the time is at hand to put a stop to this evil. This is only possible through forming national and global alliances in creating common wealth of communities, which guarantees a stake to all communities in national assets and thus staving-off poverty.

Can we ever learn? Graphic online news article: 'Greed Is Killing Africa', reports that in the early 90s a former British Premier's wealth was put at £9.5 million. The notorious dictator Kamuzu Banda's wealth was estimated at $320 million, that is 53 times that of a British Premier's.

Even more corrupt was a former Nigerian president (Abacha) who stole $1.3 billion wealth and deposited it in London and Swiss banks.

A former Zambian president (Chiluba) took the same corrupt path, stealing for self-gratification, overspending on clothes [shoes, designer suits and others-worth millions].

A 2018 Transparency International Survey (29/01/2019) – 'Sub-Saharan Africa: undemocratic regimes undermine anti-corruption efforts on corruption' - revealed an average score of just 32 for Sub-Saharan Africa (lowest index score), followed closely by Eastern Europe and Central Asia, with an average score of 35-on corruption perception. Regardless, it's inaccurate to say Africa is poor.

Africa is not poor. On the contrary, Africa is exceptionally rich but is heavily saddled by the weight of heartless and corrupt leaders - and yet infrastructure is all broken - schools and hospitals are very poorly equipped and poorly staffed. People live in abject poverty.

There is no need to blame the colonial past and the actions of imperialists for all of Africa's poverty, but the greed of Africa's political elite, which has cost Africa much more than the colonialists and imperialists took away from Africa.

The writer further cites a London Telegraph reporter, who observed that African countries' past rulers stole or misused well over £220bl. This amount is more than enough to get rid of poverty and needless suffering in Africa.

The then U.N. Secretary-General Kofi Annan – once lamented (at London press conference [2013]): "Billions of dollars of public funds continue to be stashed away by some African leaders – even when roads, health systems etc., are crumbling".

In some African countries that follow the communist path, people are blinded into believing that a failed command system in the then USSR can produce wonders in their countries. Politicians and their cronies masquerade as saints to the people and go about giving free inputs to the people in support of what they call 'command agriculture'. Guess how they do it. They give away, for example, an input pack of 25kg maize seed, 2x50kg fertilizer, 2lt of herbicide and a few more items to ice up the package. All this costing a mere $250.

For 20000 households, this adds up to $5ml. This is just a realistic example in a world where votes are bought for a song and tyranny is perpetuated. Meanwhile oligarchs, politicians and their cronies parcel out 25/30-tonner trucks of inputs for free or for a song. They even peg producer prices of the crops they grow at prices which are twice more than the global average to ensure they rake in maximum returns. This is hitting two birds with one stone in that their actions succeed in buying votes and stealing from the public purse simultaneously. All the while, the country bleeds as all this money is borrowed money that creates a black hole in the public purse. The noble writer on African greed further makes references to the Bible, citing Colossians 3:5 which equates greed with idolatry to depict the gravity of the vice.

In Europe and elsewhere in the world, Africans and other nations have sought refuge as they run away from persecution from their barbaric leaders. In the diaspora, Africans are vilified and treated in contempt and ridicule in both civil life and in the work place. It's so painful and yet many have experienced this on numerous occasions.

Most people appreciate the west's contribution in shared cultural heritage and industrialization.

But unfortunately, all the dividends are lost due to their unapologetic stance over horrific acts they committed during slavery and colonialism. Researchers and contemporary commentators label colonialists, who unjustifiably exploit other nations' resources by mayhem and bloodbath, as predatory capitalists. While the west boasts of a superior capitalist system over any other, candid researchers produced empirical evidence and argue that citizens of former colonial powers, despite affluence, are poor. To date more than 25ml American citizens are defined as poor despite affluence and the extravagance of that country. Save for gatekeepers of the capitalist system, majority of the citizens are confined to perennial benefits dependency while others lack the opportunities which the privileged few have. The guilt of slavery and colonialism seem to hang over their heads relentlessly. They don't understand why adequate education on the subject is so elusive and why their governments appear not ready to settle their reparative debt to attain remission. The confusion goes on thus precluding any sense of accomplishment in terms of social development and happiness.

The danger with predatory capitalism is that of greed and supremacy. Those involved are fearful of the opposition forces. They are paranoid and think that they must be superior to others – capable of outsmarting everyone in the sphere of

    Needless Suffering

technology, science and defense. No wonder why now the western world talks of <u>space defense force</u> to out-maneuver opponents. And yet, according to luminary figures like Mandela, the best way to be secure is by 'ensuring security of your neighbour including your opponents'. Imagine being led by headless chickens in the Tigerland wild. Such is the case when predatory capitalism controls our lives. The accidental spark of Iran /Iraq war has caused untold poverty and suffering of the citizens of those countries due to its immense devastation. I shudder to think of the Armageddon that ensues after an accidental spark of nuclear war between protagonists – and yet humankind is not taking any serious action against this looming disaster. Selfishness and military adventurism reigns. Lest we forget, any nuclear war conflagration may spell an end to our beloved human race.

At the end of the day, someone would ask if communism didn't create genius figures and made great inventions. Today we glaringly see its flaws. Wealth from predatory capitalists who masquerade as normal corporate organisations has financed inventions of novel products. But man could still archive much more when governed by just and moral norms, under a peaceful environment. It's a conundrum!

Today, predator capitalists avoid teaching their progeny the horrors of slavery and colonialism. Worse still, they are not keen to settle the reparations for their crimes. Perhaps that's why we have no peace on earth.

Western countries deliberately or through ignorance avoid conscientising their children of their countries' inhuman conquests and empire history. Failure to acknowledge history and historical obligations leads a nation into the abyss. Information influences behaviour and moulds the mind. Its absence has dire consequences. In society at large, in the work place or along the streets of London, Brussels, Madrid etc., ask if, ordinarily, western citizens understand basic African history, culture and traditions.

The average person doesn't have a clue. Quite often you would get unimaginably weird answers. Most answers point to why governments, across the western world, after slowly re-collecting a bit of their senses, are seen promoting Human Rights values, diversity, equality and anti-bulling and harassment policies. Western governments are trying to reveal the truth and act to reverse ill-treatment of Africans and other minorities.

The impeccable McGregor-Smith review (2017): Race in the workplace, gives a sickening view of the nature of discrimination. Highlights

 Needless Suffering

of the report are: 'There is discrimination and bias at every stage of an individual's career', and 'talking time is over, it's now time to act'. However, the British government acknowledges the need to 'live in a country where every person, regardless of their ethnicity or background, is able to fulfil their potential at work'. The report cites losses, well more than £24bl to the economy due to discrimination. Heart breaking in deed! Only God knows why.

Countless African and perhaps other minorities talk of harsh discrimination and ill-treatment even in universities where, for example, high quality projects, placement and written assignments are marked down because of the 'crime of their culture and skin Colour'. However, its worthy noting that even if this ugly phenomenon persists, there are (in UK and across Europe) youths, women and man of high regard, who detests discrimination in all its forms.

I blame African leaders for their greed. The same greed has precluded diasporans from investing back home because of these leaders' retrogressive policies. Only a handful of leaders are upright but many of these have been hunted down by evil forces of this world. It's heart-rending to think of how some of these upright African leaders were hunted down and got killed or made to die in exile—the likes of Thomas Sankara, Kwame Nkrumah, Patrice Lumumba and others. For fighting Apartheid, Mandela escaped death by a whisker but went on to be incarcerated for 27 years at the most notorious of all prisons – the Robben Island jail.

Contemporary Views

Some thinkers believe that no success can be achieved without some form of philanthropy (AID) to poor people, mostly in developing countries.

Dambisa Moyo, author of 'Dead Aid', however, has dismissed this view of donations or handouts as fraught with serious problems that yields negative results.

In theory, AID money helps the poor, but many Africans subscribe to Moyo's assertions in light of man's immoral ways. We throw away large amounts of food when billions go hungry every day; we stash trillions of dollars into safe heavens when the poor needs aid or when budding entrepreneurs require financial capital to start or run their businesses. Now we know that much of the AID has been given with strings attached to it. History has shown this.

Powerful forces make it impossible or difficult for people to innovate, but rather to be perpetual consumers and workers who survive on the mercy *of the capitalists. We need to employ strategic intellectual interventions in order to reverse this situation.*

Moyo laments the exploitative nature of multinationals and their governments who, through use of donors and NGOs, would pour money into unsuspecting African countries in the name of donations by way of sinking boreholes and supporting livelihood projects, water and sanitation programmes and yet behind the scenes, leaders of those recipient countries would get kick-backs in return for allowing multinationals to set up infrastructure that siphons off wealth.

Some agents would deliberately gather economic and political intelligence and transmit to their mother countries. They in turn would devise schemes using such intelligence to exploit these African countries' resource.

Why would Haiti, a precariously poor country, continue to endure such levels of poverty when the world is full of merciful donors? To understand this, let's consider what happened during colonialism, in the 19ᵗʰ and 2oth centuries. Missionaries would lead the way or move alongside agents of colonial master countries. They would preach the gospel of riches, subordination and eternal life in celestial paradise. Meanwhile these agents carved large tracks of land and pegged mines for themselves against the natives' will. They were quick to bribe

African leaders the same way they bribed them during slavery times. Most of these countries remained poor and subdued until the dawn of a sweeping revolutionary movement that brought independence and sovereignty to all African countries.

Yes, I cherish Dambisa Moyo's views on how Western Aid has fueled conflicts and induced regression in Africa. True, Western AID has fueled lots of conflicts in Africa, but inadvertently, AID is still needed in Africa a great deal to fuel up development. What is needed is appropriate AID which is unconditional and directly addresses people's needs, such as the <u>donor funded U-Dream project</u> that involved South African teenagers who built a flying plane - courtesy of the donor's support (https://www.bbc.co.uk/news/world-africa-48914418).

It's the way it is sourced into Africa which has serious flaws. Following the Keynesian Economic Model, some prudent western governments intervene sensibly to bring sanity in free markets. Equally, AID should be properly regulated by governments, albeit in sensible ways not to antagonize those who help but rather to help them direct their effort where it can yield maximum social impact.

AID agencies should not impose their programmes on people, but partner with them to solve real problems. Quite often donors merely scratch the surface of communities' problems while spending heavily on themselves at the expense of these communities.

The rapid political changes which swept across Africa has somehow brought hope to the people. These changes have been a result of the fall of Apartheid and the successful decolonization/ liberation of African countries. Regrettably, in many African countries, immediately after winning bitter liberation struggles, the same liberation leaders turned out to be populist despots - demagogues who survived on a system of patronage governance and hence causing untold suffering of ordinary people.

However, the emergence of democratic countries like Botswana, Namibia and a few others has brought the much-anticipated hope to the ordinary peoples of Africa.

Holding all other factors constant - ceteris paribus - Africa can catch-up and overtake Europe and other regions, at least in terms of quality living standards. Owing to least pollution levels abundance of natural resources, it can produce food for self and the entire planet - ad infinitum - so long it adheres to principles of Integrated Natural Resources Management. And, of course, due to sound Afro-social systems - which are evolving - Africa can regain top spot in life satisfaction and happiness indices.

The article - 'The white men who have plundered the wealth of Africa – The White Barons' – is a classical exemplary case of African greed (http://africangreed.blogspot.com/). The story horrifically consumes us as we try to understand why Africa continues to suffer as it does.

The article writer notes that for decades, the so-called "White Robber Barons" have exploited the African people and dried out African land without any remorse. In the past and up-to this day, they trade, steal, commit fraud, bribe, break sanctions, deal in arms and are doing whatever they want. Literally speaking, they rule Africa.

In part, the suffering of African people can be traced to the heartlessness of multinational corporations. Listening to stories of multinational corporations is mind-boggling. Consider 'stealing from africa' – why poverty? (https://www.youtube. com/watch?v=wnyemuiaofu&app=desktop).

In Africa and beyond, their exploitative businesses are no secret. Everyone knows how they run them and with whom. Ironically no one seems to care.

The writer awakens us to the reality that rulers of Africa feel invincible and no one can touch them nor stop them from their vices. The Barons know and understand the respective countries' leaders. The combined wealth of these Robber Barons run into several billions of dollars.

 Needless Suffering

Some of the barons financed and continue to finance insurgency in such countries as DRC, CAR and others. They have plundered precious minerals, timber and other resources. All these activities have caused untold suffering to the peoples of Africa.

Institutional perspectives

According to a United Nations report on sustainable goals, the number one goal is to end poverty in all its forms. The following facts are cited:

Extreme poverty rates have been cut by more than half since 1990. While this is a remarkable achievement, one in five people in developing regions still live on less than $1.90 a day. Poverty manifests itself in hunger and malnutrition, limited access to education and other basic services, social discrimination and exclusion as well as the lack of participation in decision-making. Only inclusive economic development ensures sustainable jobs and promote equality.

The UN report notes that most people living below the poverty line belong to two regions: Southern Asia and sub-Saharan Africa where extreme poverty rates are often found in fragile and conflict-affected countries. Every day in 2014, 42,000 people had to abandon their homes to seek protection due to conflict. In developed countries such factors as age, gender, unemployment, income generation and inability to set up economic activities, etc. defines poverty levels.

In his report on Causes of Poverty, Jaimin observes that poverty is the biggest obstacle against development in the developing world. He defines poverty as simply the inability to afford basic human needs such as clean water, nutrition, health care, clothing and shelter. Under such circumstances people have fewer resources than others within a society or country compared to worldwide averages. People fail to maintain a living standard adequate for a comfortable lifestyle.

The UN describes poverty as a denial of choices and opportunities, a violation of human dignity. It means lack of basic capacity to participate effectively in society. This also encompasses fundamental issues like having a job to earn one's living, not having access to credit, insecurity, powerlessness and exclusion of individuals in households and communities. Poverty manifests itself when people live on marginal or fragile environments, without access to clean water or sanitation.

Poor governance is largely to blame for the breakdown of law and order, inflation (due to economic mismanagement), high utility charges, punitive government taxes, unsustainably high government non-productive expenditure, landlordism, nepotism and backward infrastructure, to name but a few. Serious crimes and violence, child labour, endemic diseases, decaying moral values, homelessness and antisocial behaviour (mostly by the youths) prevail in impoverished communities.

CHAPTER FOUR

SOCIO-ECONOMIC PERSPECTIVES

Introduction

Scholars, historians, political scientists and others tend to assign socio-economic success or failure of states and individuals to various philosophical economic models, chief among them being, Socialism, Communism, Neoliberalism and Neo-Capitalism, among others. However, in general terms, people simply talk of capitalism and socialism.

Understanding Communism

Socialism (interchangeably used to describe Communism), is described by academics as a range of economic and social systems that implies social *ownership and democratic control of means of production. Proponents of this ideology - Karl Max and Fredrich Engels, in the 19th century - portrayed socialism in direct opposition to capitalism. They envisaged that socialism would eventually topple capitalism as a form of social ownership of the means of production. Economists and intellectuals argue that in practice, socialism has failed as it did in the then Soviet Union where it bred authoritarian regimes which resulted in impoverishing the people.*

Save for China and perhaps a few other socialist countries where communism has survived to this day, this ideology has been shelved in favour of capitalism or something in between capitalism and socialism. During its hey days, socialism managed to boost industrial and agricultural production in such countries as the former USSR, Ukraine and most of the Eastern European bloc countries - Poland and Yugoslavia included. They developed and became well industrialized.

The revolutionary spirit of communism was adored by many colonized countries of Africa which were quick to accept help to topple their colonizers. While the world was divided into two camps - 'West' and 'East' during the cold war days, Africa largely stood by the eastern block for liberation support from their western colonizers i.e. France, Britain, Spain, Belgium, Portugal and others. The liberation, though a blessing in disguise, was largely brutal with devastating consequences.

The struggle differed in size and scale depending on the stubbornness of the colonial rulers or the level of wealth each country possessed. The more the country's resource endowment, the harder it was to fight for the freedom. A case in point was that of Southern Rhodesia where the colonial leaders vowed, 'never in a thousand years will we hand over power to blacks. All this is indicative of how much wealth this country possessed - diamond, gold, copper, zinc, lithium - you name it, everything was there, just below the earth's surface. Other countries like Zambia, Tanzania, Botswana etc. got their freedoms much easier because then, not much wealth would be counted in these countries. No wonder if you ask Nigerians today how come they quickly got their independence, they are quick to quip, 'The British didn't know there was black gold under the soil, otherwise they wouldn't leave.

So, Africa and of course other regions like those ones in Asia and South America [Venezuela, Cuba, Peru, Chile, Brazil and others] got their independence from western colonial masters largely through the communist influence. Africa is grateful for that.

Now then, why and how did communism fail the world? Because of the impact of communism, the Western World described communism as for failed states, totalitarianism and poverty-stricken states. The root cause of the adversity cannot be over stressed – the threat to lose possession or ownership of means of production and assets and the redistribution of the assets to the poor. Because of this, the West never mentions the massive sacrifices made by the eastern communist countries especially USSR against fascism in WW2.

In the case of communist countries, poverty crept in when the fundamentals of rulership were ignored; pluralism, participatory democracy, tolerance, institutionalism etc. These facets collapsed under the weight of greedy and inept communist leadership.

Inherently, in a communist country such as the Soviet Union, censorship curtailed space for creativeness in various spheres e.g. arts, music etc. because communism valued utilitarianism above everything else, which killed the drive for human endeavor.

By coping failed communist policies, Africa, like other regions of the world, was caught up in the same trap.

Why Communism failed

In an article, 'Learning Mind' - https://www. learning-mind.com/why-did-communism-fail/, several factors are observed as key causes for the demise of communism, largely in the eastern bloc countries and more particularly in Russia, the first modern communist country. Let's look at these factors.

[a] Collectivization: Introduction   of collectivization of farms precluded individual right to private property and private farming.

Many African countries still deny full ownership of property, particularly land, to their citizens. Such land remains state property thus denying chance for users to use it as bank loan collateral, which is critical in boosting production.
During peak communist days, all the produce from farms would be equally distributed among the population. Dissenting voices were eliminated. In some African countries, under command farming system, produce is supposed to be sold to national marketing boards where in some instances low prices are offered, thus denying the farmers a chance to market on the open market for higher returns.

[b] Lake of rights: Communist Governments infringed upon people's rights - freedom of speech

and association were considered dangerous to the Communist party. Lack of artistical freedom and forced collectivization act are examples. Rights curtailment killed the human spirit to endeavor on economic and development matters.

[c] Failure to adapt: Communism failed to adapt to outside conditions such as the global economy and social changes. A lot of African countries close their eyes to what happens beyond their borders, thereby losing out and not catching up with vital international developments and stimuli.

[d] Lack of innovation: by allowing themselves to be a closed society, communists failed to evolve. Many African countries are not evolving at all. Many have been stagnant for many years.

Most African countries cannot make a bicycle or a sewing machine, because they lack innovation and creativeness. Because of their ineptitude, governments are entrapped in corruption and evil schemes which do not have any bearing in the lives of the people.

[e] Failure of Command economy: common ownership of resources killed creativeness and innovation resulting in reduced productivity. The system failed to observe demand and supply laws as well as determinants of competitiveness on the global market. Those in charge got more

resources than others thus creating great disparity. Communist countries committed atrocities against their citizens who did not embrace the communist doctrine. Arbitrary arrests and detentions were common. These vice practices are common across Africa today.

[f] Utopianism: in the Western minds, this was the society envisioned by Marx, Engels, Lenin, Stalin and others who painted a picture of glorifiable communist society, superior to other systems. Across Africa, communism-aligned countries would want to pretend to their citizens that they are running a sound political and economic system.

While salaries may differ in Africa with large severance packages paid to bosses and senior government officials, the majority are given pittance salaries and told to be content as a way of universal suffrage. In the absence of sound salaries workers do not find incentive to work harder nor innovate, leading to low productivity or stagnation.

[g] Tyranny: Almost all the communist countries that ever existed except a few, despotic leaders emerged, and this was largely due to the fact that the countries were founded on tyrannical principles. By default, people revolted against such government.

This is a common phenomenon in Africa today where people are revolting against their despotic regimes. A case in pointy is the 'Arab spring' which saw Egypt, Tunisia, Libya and others rise against their tyrannical leaders.

Communist philosophers of our time would say it's not the failure of communism but human greed which is causing inequality and the widening gap between the rich and poor. The greedy leaders have failed to conform to communist principles and plunged their countries into poverty.

Understanding Capitalism

The simplest way to understand capitalism is to view it as a system that allows private ownership and control of property and means of production. It emphasizes rule of law.

Market forces which hinges on competition, influences pricing mechanisms and coordinates supply and demand of goods and services, in conformity to the needs of society. Government plays a part of ensuring that the laws are followed, and it collects relevant taxis.

Because of competition, there is scope for challenging work and innovation, leading to enhanced productivity and production of superior products. This is what we see happening in the Western World.

Now let's look at Capitalism and see how it contributes towards suffering of the people. On the surface, we are told and can see that capitalism is responsible for the economic success of the Western World.

Unfortunately, capitalism has evolved into Global Corporate Capitalism. The world today is under the control of multinational corporations. These are powerful organisms which are akin to special breeds of people with an insatiable appetite for profit maximization. In theory, capitalism leads to surplus goods and hence creation of wealth. All countries that practice capitalism are supposed, in theory, to become rich as their companies are effective and efficient compared to the non-capitalist.

Critiques argue that if the above assertion was true, then we wouldn't have experienced the 2008 global economic collapse of nations, largely in the Western World. The 2008 economic recession rendered the much-touted success of capitalism bare. Large numbers of firms could have gone under had it not been for the mercy of governments which rescued them from collapse. Communists attribute this government behaviour to the predatory nature of capitalism. The fundamental question is, 'does capitalism shield people from poverty or inequality?' Anyone's' guess is as good as mine.

However, the truth is that there is massive levels of inequality or poverty in the developed western countries today, probably as it has always been in the past. To-date, several European countries are reeling under pernicious debts which they can hardly afford to repay unless severance concessions are made by lending institutions. Examples are Portugal, Italy, Greece and Spain - the so-called PIGS countries - caught up in this vicious trap. On average, their debts are greater than their GDPs. In other words, they are broke. Taxes are harsh in most capitalist countries and austerity is biting the citizens hard.

The predatory nature of capitalism has managed to keep the western countries going, otherwise majority of them could have gone bust in the same way some communist countries such as the former USSR succumbed to the effects of communist vices.

Because of their pursuit for profit, corporates have swallowed competitors to create more space for profit maximization.

From a socialist's point of view, this ideology has been responsible for dispossessing ordinary people of their assets such as land and other forms of means of production. A case in point is the Western World countries where majority of citizens do not own any land, which is considered a primary survival resource in Africa.

Neo-liberalism.

From a layman's point of view, Neoliberalism is merely an evolved form of Capitalism. According to Wikipediae: https://en.wikipedia.org/wiki/Neoliberalism, Neoliberalism refers to economic liberalization policies such as deregulation, austerity, free trade and privatization. These policies are meant to reduce government spending, giving rise to an increased role of the private sector in the economy and society. Whereas the post war period (1945 to 1980) was dominated by the Economic principles which allowed governments to intervene in economic policies and moderate economic activities, Neoliberalism advocated free market economy.

Neo-capitalism

Seen in good light by its proponents, neo-capitalism is an economic ideology which blends some elements of capitalism with other systems. It designates a new form of capitalism that is characterized by correcting capitalism's excess by means of the application of measures that guard over the social well-being of people.

Neo-capitalism is meant to promote economic freedoms, while observing the private property ownership of industries and companies and all this being moderated by centralized state economic planning mechanism.

Proponents of the ideology tell us that it supports a balance between economic growth, lower inflation, low levels of unemployment, good conditions of work, social assistance and good public services across the economy.

Ironically, most people still endure poverty hardships due to austerity, wherever it is applied. Capitalism has developed a culture where workers are treated as cogs in machines to generate wealth while paying little regard to their welfare.

Capitalists would want us to believe that unregulated markets bring economic success. Lack of market regulation, some commentators would say, caused the economic meltdown of 2008/9. It was only due to the manipulative nature of capitalism that governments were coerced into shady rescue deals with multinational corporations at the tax payers' expense. Meanwhile, many jobs were lost and for the remaining ones, low wages were guaranteed, making workers poorer. All the while, executives and shareholders went on to receive and declare huge profits after the recovery - much to the chagrin of suffering ordinary masses.

Neo-classical economics (supply side economics) was influenced by Jean-Baptiste Say's

Law of Markets (1803) which advocated laissez-faire economics.

According to Say, governments should not interfere with free markets, but rather let market forces dictate demand and supply of goods and services. In free-markets, he believed optimal prices for goods and services can be achieved naturally. Customers are expected to make rational decisions.

In contrast, John Maynard Keynes' General Theory of Employment, Interest and Money, argues that governments do need to intervene to stimulate demand – through expansionary fiscal policy and money printing. Perhaps this classical economic theory is the basis upon which regulation and support to the low-income consumers of Britain and other developed countries is applied to increase aggregate demand, thus boosting economic activity.

Man are continuously striving to remodel development ideas to try and come up with paths that enables society to thrive. In this conundrum there seems to be no majority in support of either communism or capitalism. Model Classical Free Market economy (in annex), may be the answer to our economic problems. Generally, predatory corporate executives don't care about the success or failure of any particular country, but only the growth and profitability of their global corporations.

A case in point is the Congolese phenomenon where corporates extract huge mineral resource wealth, while in the process, casting a blind eye to the atrocities they cause or sponsor in that country. The You-tube video- 'The Looting Machine' - depicts this sad story. (https://www.youtube.com/watch?v=N8QUgu2KrM8) Quite often they bribe their way into business, buying government officials at will. As such corporates are as good as outlaws.

The wealthy - through their corporations - are depleting, albeit at unsustainable levels, such vital resources as oil, arable land, water, minerals, forests, fish, and many others. Environmental pollution is now the order of the day.

The reporter notes that multinational corporations garner a disproportionate share of the world GDP of $63 trillion. Sadly, in many parts of the world, a worker is not able to earn a living wage, does not have a bank account nor drive a car, but can always obtain drugs, sex, and weapons.

Ironically, Bob contends that our modern TV stations and the internet, are fueled by greed for profit. They paint a picture of a progressive world moving forward in happiness, but all this in total disregard to the suffering of the poor peoples of the world, examples being those adults and children in such countries as Afghanistan, DRC, Yemen and many others, who have endured untold hardships due to human heartlessness of the global corporate empire.

In concluding this chapter, we can safely say that both socialism and capitalism have failed society, badly. This leaves mankind with the daunting task of formulating alternative economic development models. Which ones or how? Only time will tell.

Everyone who does not belong to the camp of the rich capitalists or the oligarchs of the communist world is baffled and dumbfounded as to where a solution can come from. Some people point to the success of China and attribute it to the 'dragon spirit', which is a spirit for endurance, love, law abiding and every other important virtue that makes society remain intact and focused on building its nation.

Some would jokingly say that there were similar dragons in Africa starting from the period before the Whiteman arrived but, because of tribal infighting - which bred greediness and despotism in some ethnicities, the dragon escaped to other parts of the world, perhaps to china. Contemporary thinkers suggest things could have taken a beautiful twist if the Whiteman in Africa had embraced Africans and their civilization and sought to work with them in partnership.

   Needless Suffering

Recall the great British Cecil John Rhodes who founded Rhodesia; he vowed, 'from Cape to Cairo'. In his mind he saw people working together harmoniously building railway lines that stranded the entire length of Africa from South to the North. Amazingly, that dream has not come to fruition, to this day. This could probably have developed into the 'Silk Road of Africa', but alas! What an opportunity lost.

Those who succeeded Rhodes never believed in coexisting with fellow Africans, which could have been the greatest precursor for peaceful and excellent development in Africa. Because of that approach, untold suffering and poverty engulfed the continent of Africa as natives, having run out of peaceful options for coexistence with their colonial masters, resorted to revolutionary methods which, quite often, were very brutal.

The colonialists were like beasts under the influence of Eugenics Philosophy. They paid no regard to indigenous knowledge and traditions. Ian Douglas Smith, the last White British colonial ruler in Southern Rhodesia, stated that Africans would never be allowed to rule themselves in a thousand years. Owing to a warped mind-set, Smith and his cronies could not understand that Africans had same genotype and biological make-up as any other human being. Shamefully, they would later pay a heavy price for this ignorance.

All these misconceptions were laid bare by victories of African liberation forces. By gun or through diplomacy, Africans shined and won their freedom and independence.

I wish you were in Mozambique or Zimbabwe or Angola, during the struggle days, to fully understand sacrificial spirit of Africans and how horrific the liberation wars were. During pre-independence era, in mines and farms which raked in billions of foreign currency, Africans worked for pittance wages. In some instances, they were given dried fish, beans and corn as food wage. The irony is that the settlers deliberately dislocated natives from their original mode of crop and livestock production which sustained them for tens of thousands of years. Traditional scientific knowledge on medicines needlessly got lost as settlers systematically targeted rich African traditions.

Regardless of all this dark history, Africans forgave their tormentors and today do cherish living and working together - side by side for common developmental goals. In fact, in many African countries, children of former colonial masters are coming back to find work or invest in these countries. Others seek matrimonial relationships to build families as there is little like that to talk about in western countries due to the negative effects of industrialization.

All those westerners who set foot in Africa will tell you that Africa is one of the best places to live on earth as it is endowed with rich cultural heritage and not to mention ubiquitous natural resources that nourish life in incomparable forms. Beautiful sunshine, clean fresh water, minerals and rich fauna and flora, all in abundance. British Biologist, Attenborough once described Africa's wild life as 'the greatest and most beautiful natural spectacle in the world'. Awesome! Just visit the Masai-Mara of Kenya or Mana Pools of Zimbabwe or Kruger National Park of South Africa to witness and experience unparalleled true joy of life. Or immerse yourself in African social communities and taste how real life feels. You just feel the awesome beauty of the Lord.

A lot of forces drag Africa backwards. An article carried by The Independent newspaper: 'Zim-Sino relations needs reset', cites unsustainability of relationships of individual countries that have been pursuing relationships with powerful economies such as China on a party-to-party basis.

Multilateral partnerships such as the China–Africa relationship, particularly through the forum on China-Africa Cooperation and other such platforms is the way to go.

As Africa's largest trading partner and a major investor, China's actions have huge implications for the development of the African continent.

The writer advises that Africa needs to accurately anticipate and assess the Chinese agenda, weighing the good part and downside of the relationship, always considering the people's needs. Genuine relationship with China to help Africans must lead to concrete agricultural development, industrialization, technical assistance, job creation, and technology transfer through investment in manufacturing industries, not just extraction. Africa should go for beneficiation of its vast natural resources.

In the absence of appropriate strategies, most African countries, despite owning abundant resource, could paradoxically, find themselves benefiting very little from multilateral relationships.

CHAPTER FIVE

HOPE

The Indomitable Spirit of Man

Come on citizens of the world! Dead Aid depicts Africa as a sick and hopeless continent. Bony children, who are malnourished and hopeless, are shown on television every day. The culprits are predatory NGO sharks, who relentlessly mount vicious PR-campaigns depicting Africa as in dire need for help, but for their own financial advantage. But you need to look at the salaries of NGO and donor community staff to understand their sincerity in helping Africa. Meanwhile, as this pitiable image go live on television, the most beautiful pictures of Africa are hidden from view. This has helped distort the beautiful image of Africa. Having said this, it doesn't mean the work of good AID agencies shouldn't be recognised. Great! We appreciate.

Nonetheless, time for Africa and the rest of the poor countries of the world has arrived; it's now. Beautiful cities have erupted across Africa over the past decades. Just 50 years ago no one on earth ever thought Africa would be free. But today its 100% independent. However, the scourge of poverty still lives with us due to greedy and barbaric leaders who are easily manipulated with forces of evil. Where can we grow ideal leaders?

It starts with awareness creation and conscientisation of communities of the need to emancipate themselves economically as they did politically. As defined by Ledwith (2005), "Conscientisation is the process whereby people become aware of the political, socioeconomic and cultural contradictions that interact in a hegemonic way to diminish their lives". Sufficiently conscientised people become critical thinkers. They gather and analyse fats with a view to challenge the status quo.

When people become aware of their circumstance, they take collective action to resolve their common problems.

Our youths have great potential. In this information age, we expect them to behave like any other progressive youths, creative and innovative like the third-world Chinese who are into high-tech gadgetry. For example, they now practise crop chemical application using drones, almost effortlessly.

Apart from our resilient natural environment which gives us food and most of our needs like clothing and shelter, it's the youths who carry the bigger part of the burden because they have the energy and cognitive power to do so. This is the source of our inspiration and hope. Our educated youths realise that it's not going to be by force or coercion but by applying strategic intellectual interventions, in all our endeavours.

The potential of well-educated youths of Africa in staggering. The African Development Bank report, 'Africa's Youth - The Demographic Dividend', observes that Africa has the fastest-growing and most youthful population in the world. Over 40% are under the age of 15 and 20% are between the ages of 15 and 24. The report defines demographic dividend as 'a large workforce that creates a window of investment opportunity in the education and health of their children and in technology and skills development to strengthen the economy'.

Africa now wields enormous clout, especially from its well-educated and skilled diaspora citizens. Those in the diaspora need to find one another and put heads together to network and develop their countries. It's easy to jump start Africa's Emerging Markets because, most importantly, agricultural land and infrastructure are still needing development which implies unparalleled massive employment opportunities.

It's just a case of turning problems and resources into opportunities.

Just recently a George Washington high School (opened in 1963), could express disgust about the 1600ft^2 of murals depicting the school and George Washington-the first American president-in the context of ownership of American African slaves and their inhuman treatment of Native Americans.

The 60s were characterized by the 'no Irish, no dogs and no Blacks' mentality, in UK, a clear sign of ignorance and moral bankruptcy, but this is now being reversed.

A 2016 public media report stated that Queen Marry University of London community described King Leopold as a genocidal colonialist and, on that basis, sought to remove the plaque from the university. This is encouraging as it shows that the enlightened Britons and other Europeans can now distinguish between injustice and morality. It would appear, with proper conscientisation, western societies can wake up to challenge their historical past and act to achieve restoration which should bring normalcy to world order.

Once touted as a terrorist by many western countries and their citizens before his prison release, Mandela turned out to be an icon, global states man and Peace Price Laurette just as recent as 1994 when he became president.

Developing countries should confine FDIs to complex, high capital-intensive projects, while ordinary people are helped to set-up scalable community commonwealth projects. which delivers socio-economic impact. This way we can eradicate poverty and needless suffering. Through a special Affirmative Social Enterprise model, this dream can be realized. Fascinating indeed! That's how life should move.

Progressive nations, the likes of Communist China and Scandinavian countries have already followed similar programmes that benefit the people. Their successes have been phenomenal and the envy of most countries of the world.

It is possible to create wealth with just reasonable cash capital through the art of entrepreneurship. You may ask, how? The story is told in the next part in this series. Human capital is key to unlock all the potential of our motherland. Every other resource is tied to our land. Only one thing has been letting us down, lack of will power and set-backs due to greediness of our leaders and the effects of neo-capitalism.

To ensure your own financial security, make others feel secure. It would it's also true to say that for any government to enjoy the wealth of its citizens, it should firstly empower those same citizens to generate wealth.

We have understood the root causes of our problems. Maybe we need to delve deeper for further understanding and getting clearer insights into our quagmirish situation. From a business point of view, I can say a SWOT analysis is necessary to understand our situation. Let's evaluate our strengths and weaknesses. I know there are great opportunities in a land of plenty like Africa and perhaps even more so in some other parts of the world. It's just a case of putting our act together well. Obviously, the threats are there. So long the predatory forces of human nature remain with us, we are bound to see attempts to reverse whatever gains we can make in our lifetime. For the sake of our children, we just can't give-up. Let's be on guard all the time. Controlled markets and political influences could be a great threat, among other forces. So, considering this scenario, we just need to join hands in unison and put up a fight, a strategic and tactful one. Just entering a battlefield with anger won't win us anything.

In Europe e.g. UK, it would be easier for those receiving benefits to forgo a month's taking and put that amount to a common social enterprise project. This would change their lives forever. It's possible. The same applies to those in USA. If all those 30ml-plus poor Americans could spare $100 each, they can easily set up a viable, well-resourced enterprises that can trade and generate healthy profits for the betterment of their lives.

The trouble is that the predatory forces, as seen in preceding chapters, cannot create that environment where one would be free to think. You are rather allowed to accept free handouts and keep quiet for all your life. Meanwhile you are reduced to either a beggar surviving on scraps or perpetual worker where you don't own the true means of production. You won't get involved in reasonable forms of economic participation to empower and free yourself. You won't realise any surplus for pleasure and true personal development. You will toil in hard labour for six months, for example, to raise enough money for a holiday while the oligarchs of Africa and elsewhere have multiple times more to spend.

The first approach is to think 'community' than self. What can we do as a community to help society? This is the approach that Jesus took in his entire life and career. He thought of other people than himself. All he did was for the people and in the process, he lived with the people and gave-up his life for people's sake.

This is the same reason why corporates are successful, although for some it's for wrong causes. Why! Because synergistically, individual shareholders put their resources together for common cause. The trick is that these corporates won't allow you to join their clubs on even terms and reap the benefits together with them. They can only do so in the name of free market where you 'jump in' at your own risk through buying risky shares in their companies. A few will win. The challenge is how to mobilise resources and make them work for mankind. We should turn communities into economic units for the benefit of society.

Culture Magic: Analogue of the Chinese Dragon

The Chinese success story refers to the power of the Chinese Spirit - The Chinese dragon. In their world this dragon represents the spirit of the Chinese people. Chinese dragons traditionally symbolize potency and auspicious powers particularly over typhoons, floods and other severe hazards. In other words, the dragons embody the Chinese spirit that protect the people from harm. Today, the dragon spirit is synonymous with luck and success. Inadvertently, the Chinese would also attribute their success to the defeat of the corrupt Chinese dynasty, by mid-20th Century.

Influenced by their culture, the people of China, through their government, ensures that there is accountability, transparency and participatory democracy involving the people. People are involved in the running of their country. They always consider business logic, social and environmental impact in whatever decision they take. Those who run government are answerable to the people. Harsh punishment is meted to thieves and corrupt officials. Government supports people in their endeavours in various projects and development activities. They call it 'Socialism with Chinese characteristics'.

These are a few of the many factors that have propelled China into position two on the global development stage. These are the good governance factors missing in most countries of the world.

People simply need help in understanding the root cause of their problems. After this phase they further need assistance in setting up livelihoods programmes so they can work for their lives and families in an equal and fairer society.

CHAPTER SIX

HAND OF GOD REVEALED

Our eyes are so closed we can't discern reality. Whereas affirmative community commonwealth projects are a novel initiative that can address poverty, just a handful of governments are keen to support this idea.

The case for community social enterprises is revealed by Winnie Byanyima, Executive Director for Oxfam International, who, in her pre-2019 Davos report (The shocking truth about inequality today- https://www.weforum. org/agenda/2019/01/the-shocking-truth-about-inequality-today/), observes that corrupt governments fail to clamp down on tax dodging by wealthy people and corporations, resulting in loss of around $170bl a year in poor countries.

Ironically, the same governments outsource to connected private companies, vital poverty-busting public services such as healthcare and education while excluding the poor. The concept of community commonwealth projects teaches us that such services should serve as the foundations on which people can work their way out of poverty and yet they are being taken away from them (the people).

Winnie concludes by giving a bleak picture that mirrors 10000 people who are dying daily for want of healthcare-a result of poor government policies.

Miracles do Happen

After 1994, various media houses reported how an emphasis on neoliberalism values (not necessarily morals), helped in the release of Nelson Mandela from Apartheid prison. The passion for free markets prompted a British premier to concede to capitalists who agitated for the release of Mandela in exchange for business success. This led to lifting of sanctions and brought an end to Apartheid system. For many years predating 1994, the common Euro-mantra was negative of Mandela, only to change at the appointed time when they saw the statesmanship in the icon - a unique hero and Nobel Peace Prize laureate, who contributed so much in changing the course of history.

The same British Premier had earlier in 1979 initiated the Lancaster House Conference which ended a very pernicious revolutionary war in Zimbabwe. May peace be upon her spirit. Commonwealth members, whose businesses had suffered heavily from the realities of war in Rhodesia, lobbied the premier to play a part in ending this war to save businesses. Perhaps not from the view point of the evils of colonialism.

Even Robert Mugabe, the once famous revolutionary leader, who led Zimbabwe to its independence from Great Britain, was ecstatic in disbelief, quipping: 'We never saw it coming'. 'In fact, we were planning for a 'harder push', thinking we still needed a few more years to achieve victory'. In fact, we were planning for a 'harder push', thinking a few more years of struggle and sacrifice were still needed'. God's power is awesome. Images of 1978 Zambia bombings of refugee camps by Rhodesian forces and the similar 1976 Nyadzonia refugee bombings in Mozambique are nerve racking (https://www.youtube.com/ watch?v=dzJfy5z5gj4 and https://www.youtube. com/watch?v=1vn4LHcr938&list=PLJiMEJgqQ-RimZ7pCqp_sAaLqTdSS7keM&index=7) While in Zimbabwe, seeing military jets flying these missions, is something that changed my view of reality.

The videos are harrowing and nerve racking. 'Africa's Liberation wars' on You-tube give conclusive facts.

Miracles do happen indeed! Just visualize a brutal war in which everyone hopes for its end, and you are told: 'The war has ended'. True, miracles do happen! Liberation wars of Africa and the total independence of Africa has, in deed, turned a chapter in the global civilization history.

We are lucky to have witnessed some of these sacrifices in living memory. The miracle was that the cold war prompted the Eastern bloc countries (USSR, Romania, the then Yugoslavia, Poland, Bulgaria and others who formed the Warsaw Pact, which sought to spread Socialism, to oppose the capitalist grouping of NATO of the west, by supporting liberation movements of colonised African countries. They succeeded.

Who ever thought slavery would end after more than 300 hundred years? Industrialisation by the turn of the nineteenth century meant human labour could be replaced by machinery. Coupled with the rise in cost of suppressing slave uprising, the appetite for slave blood rescinded, rendering slavery less attractive. The suppressive attitude against abolitionists waned. This invigorated brave Britons to campaign for abolition of slavery and succeeded. So, in a way slavery was brought to an end not because man could reason morally but by circumstances in the factors of industrialisation and personal sacrifice of slaves. Amazing indeed! Isn't it?

John Wesley, the celebrated preacher and founder of the Methodist Church and several dozen others, the likes of James Beattie (1735-1803),

Anthony Benezet (1713-1784), Elizabeth Blackwell (1821-1910) and William Fox (1791-1794) campaigned selflessly against slave trade and succeeded. Slavery was finally abolished in Great Britain and most of its colonies through the Slavery Abolition Act of 1833. Liberia was allowed to gain freedom and become a place for freed slaves in 1847.

Across the Atlantic, the Emancipation Proclamation was issued by US President Abraham Lincoln on 22 Sept 1862 and came into force by 1Jan 1863. Thirteenth amendments to the Constitution of the United States was proposed by 31 Jan 1865.

The amendment stated that: 'Neither slavery nor involuntary servitude, except as a punishment for crime whereof the party shall have been duly convicted, shall exist within the United States, or any place subject to their jurisdiction.' Ratification of the thirteenth amendment was completed by 6 Dec 1865. This was the precursor for modern day Civil Rights movement. God is merciful.

The General Assembly of the United Nations adopted Universal Declaration of Human Rights on 10th Dec 1948. Article 4 states: 'No one shall be held in slavery or servitude; slavery and the slave trade shall be prohibited in all their forms.'

The Cold War also contributed towards attainment of some peace and freedoms. At the height of Colonialism, the Almighty Lord struck Europe with the plague of WW2 of 1939-45. It became so devastating that, literally speaking, it economically sucked-dry most of Africa's former colonial powers i.e. Britain, France, Belgium, Italy, Spain, Portugal, Germany etc. Some became insolvent. Economic malaise meant colonialists couldn't keep up with their commitments including cost of running colonies. Their grip on colonies was forever loosened.

Most African countries and many others across the world such as India, got independence after WW2. With the Soviet Union's support, in 1949 the CCP won the Chinese Civil War and established the People's Republic of China. Amazingly, China would go on to help most colonised African countries (e.g. Zimbabwe, Angola, Mozambique, South Africa etc.) to free themselves from the burden of colonialism. Early to be freed in the 50s were Libya, Sudan, Morocco and many others. 1957 Ghana independence from Britain reinvigorated the quest for independence across Africa. Nkrumah, the first Ghanaian president vowed, 'Only when the whole of Africa attains freedom, will Ghana be free'.

After Africa attained its freedom, the cold war ended. This was signified by the fall of the communist super power king-pin — the USSR (which followed the Marxist Communist

Doctrine). Clearly, the USSR disintegrated after accomplishing the task of helping Africa free itself from the yoke of colonialism and this exemplifies the miraculous hand of our creator. The Chinese Communist Party (CCP) and its leader Mao's Zedong's victory over the Nationalists on Oct 1949 was a blessing to the African independence cause as China would graduate to become the major contributor in supporting liberation of colonised African states. The birth of modern China in 1949 is one of the benefits of WW2 as it taught the Chinese, like other nations, that tyrannical and even colonial regimes could be defeated and get removed from power. Today, ordinary Africans - like many from other regions, applaud the Chinese for their unwavering support to the poor countries but do detest its (Chinese's) blind eye on undemocratic and dictatorial regimes.

Due to the communist influence, several countries waged struggles to gain independence and succeeded. The Russians, Chinese, Bulgarians and many other communist countries supplied simple but advanced weaponry that taught colonialists an everlasting lesson – that predation has no place in human society. And yet today, communism has lost its luster and is shunned by most countries of the world. Amazingly, the advanced Scandinavian countries also supported the liberation struggles with humanitarian materials e.g. clothing and/or combat uniforms and food.

With the exception of Ethiopia and Egypt, which had circumstantially received their independence before WW2, the rest of African countries got their independence after WW2, thanks to the punishing impact of this great war.

The Portuguese 'Revolution of the Generals' of 1975 loosened Portugal's grip on its colonies, giving rise to the independence of Guinea Baseu, Soa Tome, Angola and Mozambique. In the 60s, Senegal, Madagascan, Burkina Faso, Guinea and many others further gained independence from France. The British also couldn't hold on to its colonies and ceded power to Somaliland in 1960 and to Zambia, Kenya and Tanzania in 1964 while Zimbabwe achieved its own by 1980.

Much of the independence was won through diplomatic negotiations. Trouble arose in countries of rich pickings, the likes of South Africa, Rhodesia, Mozambique, Angola and others with endowments of high value recourses such as minerals - copper, gold, diamonds etc., and fertile agricultural land. In these countries serious battles would be fought to gain independence. Rhodesia was so attractive in resources so much so that the Rhodesian leaders, led by Ian Douglas Smith, reneged and unilaterally declared independence

(UDI) from British on 11 Nov of 1965. Little did they know this was a precursor for excruciating sanctions by Britain. In response to circumvent sanctions, Rhodesia innovated immaculately in all spheres including in industry and agriculture. Economically, it achieved a place in the top five richest countries of Africa.

At its peak in the late 70s, Rhodesia exported more than 800 industrial products to selected markets in Africa and the whole world. Exports of highest tobacco quality and minerals [gold, nickel etc.] was achieved. Rhodesia was branded the breadbasket of Africa as it became a continental leader in production of food crops. But sanctions remained and the liberation war ensued unabated, giving rise to the Lancaster House Conference which ushered independence. It was a turn for Britain to fight back the UDI and its proponents. Margaret Thatcher, the then British premier instructed the protagonists to go for democratic elections. For Smith, it was a case of jumping from a frying pan into the fire as he knew democratic elections would end his political life. In his book entitled, 'Bitter Harvest: The Great Betrayal', Smith bemoans the British for hamstringing him into handing over the highly priced Rhodesia to native Africans. Of cause, in the ensuing elections of 1980, Rhodesia became independent.

To-date, all 55 African counties are free and independent from colonialism. However, still intact is neo-capitalism.

Regardless, the freedom of Africa from the yoke of colonialism and imperialism is the 'miracle of our time'. The merits compel us all to celebrate, if at all we are sufficiently civilised, with enough intellectual capacity to discern reality.

CHAPTER SEVEN

CONCLUSION - THE CHALLENGE OF OUR TIME

Ending poverty and needless suffering has become ever more a daunting challenge of our time. We should be ashamed when we see our brothers in the developed world spend scare resources affluently. Some leaders go on to ignite wars, so they make money by selling weapons in complete disregard to human suffering. Wars due to greed have caused the displacement of millions of people across the globe.

According to a UNICEF report, around 22,000 children die each day due to poverty. Hunger, lack of sanitation and access to clean water and inadequate health care facilities are the main factors. Close to 1 billion people still couldn't read and write by the dawn of 21st century.

Without any shadow of doubt, the world is short of prudent leaders and people who can conceive brilliant ideas to stem needless suffering of the people by way of creating projects which leads to creation of jobs and sustenance of sound livelihoods.

As we talk, millions of Masai people look and watch government and capitalists set up infrastructure in their territories, the so-called investments in safaris and the hospitality industry in general. Meanwhile these Masai people are not involved but they know in their minds they also deserve a fair share of the cake. The same applies to the native Amazonians in whose lands oil companies have set up infrastructure to exploit the resource without involving the local natives. In all cases, they share profits with these countries' governments and their officials while very little if anything at all goes to the source areas.

Consider the Kibera Slums of Kenya; it's as if there is no government. It doesn't take $5bl to turn around life of the Kibereans if there is human will power.

The level of greed, corruption and suffering of people globally, may compel one to think that perhaps we have entered the final phase of the earth's existence as per fulfilment of end-time prophesies.

Community Commonwealth programmes represent a special Social Enterprise movement where ordinary people take a stand to compel their governments to invoke affirmative action that addresses the absence of empowerment projects in society.

However, not all time is lost. We can still reverse the current social order if we work in unison, discovering and conscientizing one another on the challenges of our time. This is the time we need man and women of superior intellectual power; the youths and those in their prime who can formulate economic models that embraces Smithsonian philosophies and work for the success of society. In this information age where people are moving to think like intelligent objects, it is critical that we work together, networking and collaborating as nations or individuals to exploit the best of our minds in terms of inventing products and services that offer the best for our lives. An African 'prophet' once talked of a 'Dream to Reality: a United States of Africa', pointing out at the unparalleled enormous economic potential which Africa has. The dark forces working against Africa are also mentioned.

The challenge is to think intuitively like great people, who, in our time, have produced such great products as the computer and the internet, that have dramatically changed our lives and the course of history. The 'tsunami' of information via social media – 'What's-up', 'Instagram', 'Twitter' etc., is more of a miracle than anything else. Despots and predators can no longer hide behind their fingers as they loot global resources while they care less for the poor.

We need sound econometric models that treats the economy as a tame-beast, that is capable - when nourished well - to provide for all. Such a system, founded on efficient and fair taxation regimes, will stimulate economic activities leading to enhanced productivity that spurs exports and domestic consumption. Commerce and industry will grow. In fact, pretty much every sector will be positively affected. Stewardship wages are earned while every adult is supported to gain a stake in various scalable community commonwealth ventures, that will grow to match or outcompete FDIs.

For our economies to be vibrant and viable, we need high aggregate demand of goods and services by a critical mass of financially powerful consumers. This is achievable. We need a change of culture and the way we perceive reality.

A change in socio-cultural focus should enable UK, a former great empire and leader in slavery, take a lead in working for global peace. The UK Civil Service and private sector are marvelous but their effectiveness can only be valuable if their services meaningfully impacts the poor.

Whatever the case is, now is the time to embrace each other and work together as one global family, complementing each other's efforts. Even those nations with reparation obligations can, in good faith, act to redeem themselves by engaging members of our global community, including legal experts and donors who are ready to help them settle their moral obligation. Wisdom teaches us that it's folly to run away from one's obligations. For how long can predatory capitalists and former slave trading nations remain blind-folded to their obligations? If so, to achieve what? Like fiat currency, any wealth built from spilled blood, as a result of evil practices, will add-up to nothing, but punishment.

We ought to focus on doing more for society. We have seen that in most cases we cannot leave anything to our governments as they are part and parcel of the cabal that's bent on exploiting us. They treat us like cogs in a wheel; as machines devoid of any human feelings. But we know that the simplest economic success approach is the 'common purse model' i.e. mobilizing resources for a common cause and hence 'together each achieves more'. Let's go for it!

In all fairness, people should peacefully pursue happiness, which is the essence of creation. This is probably possible when all nations, small and large, acknowledge the consequential impact of the evil system man has created. Oligarchs, predatory capitalists and despotic oppressors should have no place in our civilised society.

 Needless Suffering

Global powers should desist from military adventurism but rather promote global peace. Let's forge ties in our globalised village and trade freely as diverse, inclusive and respectable nations, for the benefit of mankind. Let's make our time the age of peace and hope. Our yard stick should be synonymous with morality and the pursuit of peace and justice.

There is no singular factor to the realization of peace and prosperity of man on earth. Everything counts, especially affirmative action by all governments towards their citizens in order to eradicate poverty and needless suffering. This is achieved through empowering the people so they gain true emancipation. The aim of every community should be Environmental Stewardship and pursuit of Sustainable Integrated Resources Management that will support the needs of present and future generations.

Elitism, predatory capitalism, greed, immorality and unjust social systems are the identified enemies of the people. In order to win, we ought to adopt a Human Rights approach to poverty eradication by revisiting the morality doctrine and encouraging governments to enact pro-poor laws that support inclusive community commonwealth endeavours.

The ball is in our court – all of us. Nelson Mandela would say: 'Fools multiply when wiseman are silent'.

Do you have to remain blind-folded with hands tied-up on food hand-outs or meagre donations? Would you watch from the terraces or choose to be a follower or laggard? No, no - you are an INNOVATOR. Action, and action indeed! It's time for action, for the sake of our children and future generations.

Strong believers and those who stand by faith and hope, the time is at hand - let's take our stand - for the sake of future generations.

ANNEX

Model Classical Free Market Economy vs Predatory Capitalism

Model Capitalism	Predatory Capitalism
Vision: economic prosperity & creating synergies - 'together each achieves more'	Strongly believes in Predator-prey relationship; good at using fiat money to acquire assets.
Synonymous with Classical Economics; Socialist Capitalism	Synonymous with Neo-liberalism and Neo-Capitalism; exploits poor people/nations
Supports government in terms of [a] Regulatory frameworks [b] Institutional frameworks	Cheats and dodges regulations and institutional requirements; bribes governments and institutions to oil their pathway in doing business.
Involved in Corporate Social Responsibility (CSR) & poverty alleviation programmes	CSR is undertaken not in good faith but to hood-wink society and governments
Pays fair taxes, not a tax dodger	Dodges taxes, stashes wealth in safe havens
Pays modest wages to workers	Underpays workers to maximise profits
Engages international partners in a win-win approach in business undertakings	Predates and preys on unsuspecting nations by exploiting their resources
Supports development of SMEs including Social Enterprises (SE)	Views SE and SMEs as threats and hence offers little or no support
Plays positive part in globalisation issues e.g. environment, Human rights etc	Pays little attention to environmental issues; not keen to act on obligations
Breeds statesmen	Breeds oligarchs and impoverishes society. Evil
Synonymous with peace, development and social happiness	Synonymous with wars, suffering and poverty Breeds unkind and super rich people
Shared leadership and shared vision are paramount ingredients.	Made up of narrow section of population - self-serving clique of elites who dominate government and culture.
Promotes E&D & empowerment for all.	Rewards the privileged few.
Promotes participatory democracy	Thrives on ignorant citizenry

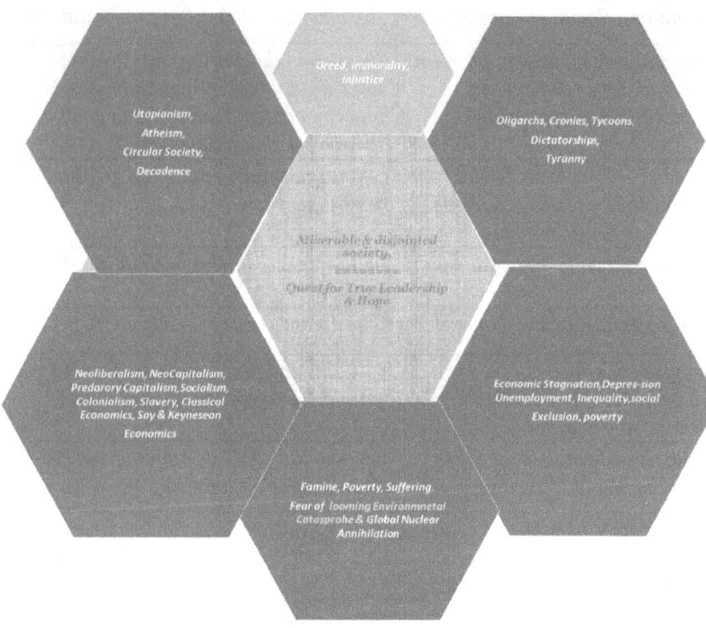

The Conundrum

www.ingramcontent.com/pod-product-compliance
Lightning Source LLC
Chambersburg PA
CBHW051459250726
48655CB00001B/502